Kick Start Your Care

For new graduates, the key challenge remains how to secure that first career-related job. Full of guidance and tips on how to handle the complex field of job hunting, *Kick Start Your Career* can help navigate an ever-changing job market and secure your chance at your desired career. It is a valuable investment in your future. It advises the reader on how to:

- stand out in job applications;
- use social media for job searching;
- create resumes and cover letters that stand out;
- succeed at interviews.

It provides a practical, hands on, step-by-step approach. With an integrated Personal Plan that helps create key job search documents it directs soon-to-be graduates towards achieving their career aspirations. Accompanying online resources include examples and templates, which can be downloaded in Word format to help you prepare resumes and other job search documents.

This book will help graduates progressively build up job-hunting resources – skills, achievements, resume, cover letter and interview responses – and turn this into a practical outcome: a new job. It is a key companion to any student or recent graduate exploring the job market.

Lee Smith's professional life included developing young graduates. He holds multiple qualifications in applied science and technology. Extensive experience in preparing Personal Development programmes led to a focus on helping young graduates transition from university to find their first career job.

John van Genderen is Professor Emeritus at the University of Twente, the Netherlands, and International Visiting Professor at Wuhan University, China. He has carried out education and training programmes at universities worldwide. He has also assisted numerous young graduates in finding suitable employment both at home and abroad.

'This book helps graduates manage the dramatic change from a university environment into a professional career. The book's guidelines and assistance are very helpful. *Kick Start Your Career* supports the goal of university that graduates are successful in finding a career job. It is a valuable resource for graduates. Highly recommended!'

Dr.-Ing. Christine Pohl, *University of Osnabrueck,*
Germany

'Students are continually looking for information, knowledge and skills that will set them apart from others in the job market. This publication will provide that resource ... and fills a very significant gap that should have global interest.'

Professor Stuart Phinn, *The University of Queensland,*
Australia

'The book provides practical guidance to students on how to secure the right job in an increasingly global market. It provides insights into employment opportunities in USA, UK, Europe, Asia and other regions, and strategies to successfully join the dynamic international workforce.'

Professor Anupma Prakash, *University of Alaska*
Fairbanks, USA

'The change from a university environment into a professional career is quite dramatic. Studying is different from working. Different responsibilities, initiatives to design work flows, etc. create a lack of confidence. The identification of own capabilities and potential that could match a suitable job is a challenge. Often graduates are not used to selling themselves and stand for their talents and possibilities. This book will be an invaluable companion to all new graduates.'

Professor Ochir Altansukh, *National University of*
Mongolia, Mongolia

'This book aims to encourage and help young graduates. It does just that. This is so important at a critical stage in the life/career of graduates after investing so much into attaining a degree. It is also valuable in that it encourages and provides alternate career options and support at a tough time.'

Matthew McDade, *Australia*

Kick Start Your Career

Successful Strategies and
Winning Techniques

Lee Smith and John van Genderen

Routledge
Taylor & Francis Group

LONDON AND NEW YORK

First published 2018
by Routledge
2 Park Square, Milton Park, Abingdon, Oxon OX14 4RN

and by Routledge
711 Third Avenue, New York, NY 10017

Routledge is an imprint of the Taylor & Francis Group, an informa business

© 2018 Lee Smith and John van Genderen

British Library Cataloguing-in-Publication Data
A catalogue record for this book is available from the British Library

Library of Congress Cataloging-in-Publication Data
Names: Smith, Lee, 1948- author.
Title: Kick start your career / Lee Smith, John L van Genderen.
Description: 1 Edition. | New York: Routledge, [2018] |
Includes bibliographical references and index.
Identifiers: LCCN 2017018243 (print) | LCCN 2017020383 (ebook) |
ISBN 9781315158532 (eBook) | ISBN 9781138067547
(hardback: alk. paper) | ISBN 9781138067660 (pbk.: alk. paper) |
ISBN 9781315158532 (ebk)
Subjects: LCSH: Job hunting. | Social media. | CYAC: Vocational guidance.
Classification: LCC HF5382.7 (ebook) | LCC HF5382.7.S655 2018 (print) |
DDC 650.14–dc23
LC record available at https://lccn.loc.gov/2017018243

ISBN: 978-1-138-06754-7 (hbk)
ISBN: 978-1-138-06766-0 (pbk)
ISBN: 978-1-315-15853-2 (ebk)

Typeset in Optima
by Sunrise Setting Ltd, Brixham, UK

Visit the eResources: www.routledge.com/9781138067660

Contents

Starting your career!

Congratulations – you have just graduated or are about to graduate. An exciting career waits ahead, or does it? Universities provide education, but is this enough for graduates to win a career-related job?

What then is required to secure that job? What knowledge and new skills are required? How does the job market work? What opportunities exist and how to find them? What role does social media play in job searching and how to use it?

A wide range of questions come to the fore: how to stand out in a competitive market; how to prepare a resume and cover letter that will make an impact; and how to handle interviews so there is a job offer.

Job hunting is a new challenge for graduates. Most books provide information and leave it to the reader to try and work out how to apply it. This book is different. It is based on helping graduates develop their Personal Plan for securing a job. This converts information into actual practical outcomes. It will provide the material you will need for job applications such as a resume, social media bio, cover letter and interview preparation.

The aim of this book is to help young graduates navigate the job hunting marketplace and succeed in getting their first career-related job.

Collaboration note and about the authors

The origin of the collaboration by the authors in this book was a common commitment by them both to meet a need: to help graduates handle the major challenges of job hunting. And to succeed!

The collaboration encompasses the practical experiences of the authors in guiding young graduates towards their first career job. It builds on a lifetime of experience of both authors in the academic and university side through to the management side of government and private sectors. It covers all aspects of winning a job – from the graduate's perspective to understanding the prospective employer's perspective. The expert advice of other specialists is incorporated to provide valuable insights. The authors provide the bridge to help you, the graduate, make a positive transition to a new job.

Lee Smith

Lee's professional qualifications (Honours degree, professional registration, post-graduate diploma and Master's degree) are in applied science and technology. They have extended, via his management roles, to training and development of young professionals.

After completing his Bachelor of Surveying (Hons) from the University of New South Wales, Australia, he transitioned to professional registration. Post-graduate studies at the International Institute for Geo-Information Science and Earth Observation (ITC), the Netherlands followed. He completed a Masters of Applied Science (Research) degree at the South Australian Institute of Technology. Lecturing at a tertiary institution provided further understanding of the transition for graduates from university to employment.

Lee's professional career has spanned different levels of government, the private sector and international organisations. It has encompassed senior management roles where the recruitment and development of young professionals was important.

His passion in the area of personal development led to coordinating a diverse range of courses, including writing and training, to build the personal skills of others. The structure and success of this programme has contributed to the book. This book encompasses the practical wisdom and guidance that Lee has accumulated over 40 years.

Lee's commitment to helping young graduates successfully win their career jobs is the motivation behind the book.

Professor (Em.) Dr John van Genderen

Professor van Genderen's career and qualifications have extended to technology transfer, training and development of students in their chosen careers. His qualifications come from Australia, the Netherlands and the UK; they provide a wider perspective on the goals of the book.

His career has encompassed international projects in over 140 countries around the world. This has resulted in a deep understanding of the challenges of job searching across different cultures and countries. He has helped not only graduates from Western countries find suitable employment, but also many students from developing countries to find a job outside of their own country, based on first-hand practical knowledge of the cultural, language and other differences in applying for a job.

Professor van Genderen has published an extensive number of professional papers (see Google Scholar or Research Gate). He has won many international awards for his work in education and training.

After completing his BA (Hons.) in Geography from the University of Queensland, Brisbane, Australia, he completed his MSc in Delft, the Netherlands and his PhD was obtained from the University of Sheffield in the UK.

His professional career has included technology marketing in the UK, Belgium, the Netherlands and USA. His academic career involved lecturing and professorial roles. This included developing and guiding students in universities in the UK and in the Netherlands. He has been a visiting professor in many universities in China, Mongolia and Malaysia, as well as in many universities in Europe, Africa, the Middle East and in North and

South America. He is currently an Emeritus Professor at the University of Twente, the Netherlands.

He has published many papers on education, training and technology transfer, and given numerous workshops, seminars and training courses to young people. He is committed to helping young graduates to win their career job. This book reflects that goal.

Preface

Bridging from university to employment can be a challenge for graduates. The key goal becomes winning a job in your desired career area.

This book is a resource to help make that transition; to equip you with practical skills and guidance for successful job searching. It is intended to be a practical book rather than an academic treatise; to deliver positive results for you, the graduate. It is a hands-on guide. It has an international perspective, covering job hunting aspects in numerous countries.

The authors have used a Personal Plan approach to maximise the outcomes for the graduate. At the end of each chapter, the Personal Plan converts the book's guidance into your action plan. It is the basis for your successful job search preparation and job hunting.

It will help you understand how the job market operates and how to use it to your advantage. It draws on the accumulated expertise of the authors as well as expertise from other specialists to provide valuable guidance and tips that work.

Social media is a key part of modern job hunting. The book outlines job hunting techniques using social media platforms such as LinkedIn, Facebook, Twitter and Google Plus. It will help you set up your online profiles (bios) and tips to help locate the right job. You will build your job application resume and cover letter so they make a positive impact. Your interview skills will be enhanced based on tips from specialists. Your job hunting techniques will be improved.

Job markets change constantly. The book will help you handle these changes better. It will help you explore alternate job options and ways to widen your job opportunities.

Job hunting can involve complex choices. Decision support tools have been included to assist you in career choices and to enable you to make sound decisions.

The Appendices: Resources contain practical resource material and examples. The Appendices: Personal Plan will be progressively completed as you progress through the book. This becomes a key foundation resource for your job applications.

Further valuable resources are available through Routledge's website for this book: eResources. It contains appendices, templates and examples. Many of these can be downloaded in digital Word format, which you can then edit for your job application. It builds the materials you will need for winning your first career job.

This book aims to equip you to move into your first career related job. It presents successful strategies for job search preparation and winning techniques for securing a job.

We wish you well in your search for employment and a successful career.

Lee Smith
John van Genderen

Who will use the book

How to use it?

Who will use it?

The book is intended for use by a range of people. It is for:

- **Students** about to graduate.
- **Graduates** seeking their first career-related job.
- **Job seekers** encountering challenges in finding a job and wanting to improve their job hunting skills.
- **Universities** seeking a resource to assist their students to transition to employment.
- **Career advisors** seeking to assist graduates in job hunting.
- **Employment professionals** as a resource to assist their clients seeking a new job.

How to use the book?

How to use the book?

The book is designed to help readers in a number of ways:

- **Self-tailored guidebook** to allow students to apply the advice via the Appendices: Personal Plan; it will build the resources graduates will need for job searching (achievements, resume, job application cover letter, online social media profile, etc.).

- **Detailed contents** to allow readers to revisit chapters or directly access parts (e.g. interview preparation). This includes an index, contents, eResources, overview and chapter-by-chapter abstracts.

- **Group discussions/tutorials** are contained in a number of chapters for those who would use the book and its material for a course.

- **Resources** are provided in the Appendices with practical resource examples (resumes, job application cover letter, etc.).

- **eResources:** use the eResources website for the book to access valuable supplementary resources in digital format. It includes templates and examples, such as resumes and cover letters that can be downloaded in digital Word format.

- **References** are provided at the end of each chapter and there are additional literature references and some useful websites for further study on each of the topics treated in that chapter. These are also available via eResources: Web References as clickable links.

- **Whole book or fast-track?** Life is busy and time is short, so we often struggle with time to do the things we need or want to do. The book has been set up to allow you to work through the whole programme or fast-track a shorter option, or just check out key chapters relevant to your job search situation.

eResources: added digital resources

eResources are available via Routledge's website for this book. These include: Appendices, Resources and Templates. In particular readers can download the Appendices: Personal Plan and Templates in digital Word format, which will assist in compiling job application materials.

To access eResources

Search/Go to: Routledge Text Books or www.routledge.com/

Search window: type "Your Career": it will then take you to the eResources for this book.

Or you can access the eResources via the short cut: https://tinyurl.com/kyxnfaq

The eResources will provide access to:

- Overview: eResources
  - eResources overview: contents
  - How to use eResources
- Appendices
  - Resources
    - Resumes/CVs resources and examples
    - Cover letter examples
    - Resume examples for different countries
  - Personal Plan

- Templates
  - Resumes/CVs
  - Free resumes
  - Resumes: countries
  - Cover letter
- Decision tools
  - SWOT analysis (strengths, weaknesses, opportunities and threats)
  - Decision balance analysis
  - Force field analysis
- Web references

Full programme or fast-track?

You can use the full programme (whole book), a fast-track option or focus on particular topics.

Whole book

The full programme seeks to provide a wide view of job hunting and getting you, the graduate, prepared for the job search. Follow the stages in the book through the chapters and Appendices: Personal Plan. Just do one step at a time and it will all come together.

Fast-track

Our lives are busy, so sometimes we just want to focus on the key aspects. It will not have the same flow or comprehensiveness, but the fast-track option will deliver some results. How can you do this with this book?

The fast-track stages you could focus on are:

Chapter 1: Getting prepared

- Introduction to job hunting.

Chapter 4: Job hunting – key factors

- Important factors to help you win a job.

Chapter 5: Locating job opportunities

● Where to look; understanding the job market and the role of social media.

Chapters 6–8: Social media

● Understanding social media in modern-day job hunting. How to use LinkedIn, Facebook, Google Plus and Twitter for job hunting.

Chapters 12–13: Foundation resume (Stages 1 and 2)

● Building a resource of your skills, education, attributes and experience.

Chapter 14: Referees and references

● How to use referees to win that job.

Chapter 15: Preparing your targeted resume: country-specific

● Editing your foundation resume to a short version that is region- or country-specific.

Chapter 16: Preparing your tailored cover letter

● Building a convincing cover letter to win an interview.

Chapter 17: Interview preparations

● How to present well in an interview.

These are the core chapters.

Going deeper

The following chapters can be explored to allow you to go deeper in your job search preparations.

Chapter 2: Adaptable strategies

- Learning how to adapt to changes in the job market.

Chapter 3: Personal abilities

- Developing personal abilities such as adaptability, resilience and endurance to help you in the job hunt; techniques to encourage you.

Chapter 9: Personal development

- Understanding yourself; tools to help handle complex decisions.

Chapter 10: General Achievements

- Developing short statements on your achievements; responding to requirements such as teamwork, communication and people skills, etc.

Chapter 11: Achievements Extended

- Responding to job- and profession-specific criteria in your job application.

Abbreviations

Bio: Short for biography or profile. An outline of a person's skills, education and experience.

CBT: Cognitive behavioural therapy. A psychological technique. It is based on how we think, how we feel and how we act.

CV: Curriculum Vitae. An outline of a person's skills, education, references and contact details. It is used in job applications to outline an applicant's suitability for a position. Also called a resume. In some countries, CV refers to a longer resume for academic positions.

EU: European Union. A political and governmental body that links signatory nations in Europe.

HR: Human resources.

MBTI®: Myers-Briggs Type Inventory®. An evaluation methodology for a person's personality type.

NZ: New Zealand.

NGOs: Non-government organisations. Covers non-profit and voluntary groups. They are independent from government organisations.

SII®: STRONG interest inventory (SII)®. An evaluation methodology of a person's interests.

SOARL: An acronym to develop achievement statements. It represents: (S) situation; (O) objective; (A) action; (R) results; (L) learning.

SOLER: An acronym for our posture at interviews. (S) square; (O) open; (L) lean forward; (E) eye contact; (R) responsive.

UK: United Kingdom. Includes England, Scotland, Wales and Northern Ireland.

url: Uniform resource locator. Also called a web address. It allows links via the World Wide Web or Internet. Usually http:// followed by the host name, such as www.example.com, and this can be followed by a filename. A url can be: www.example.com/ index.html

US: United States.

USA: United States of America.

Acknowledgements

A book of this type involves contributions and support from many sources. The authors would like to thank our wives, Irene and Jois, for their patience and support in the long journey to prepare this book.

Thanks to Ric Benson for an understanding of personal development techniques; in particular, the Personal Plan approach to improve learning and personal development.

We would like to thank Amy Laurens at Taylor and Francis for her encouragement in making this publication possible.

We appreciated editorial management by Sharon Nickels at Sunrise Setting. The copyediting thoroughness of Hannah Turner at Turner Editorial Services was greatly appreciated and enhanced the book.

Our appreciation goes to Laura Hussey, Alexander Atkinson, Sophia Levine and the editorial team at Taylor and Francis for their support, hard work, encouragement and contributions.

1 Getting prepared

1.1 Introduction

A key challenge for new graduates is making a positive transition from tertiary studies to their first career-related job. It is the first stage of finding career-related employment and building a successful career. Our aim is to help students acquire the job search preparation and job hunting skills to achieve this.

Acquiring the education provided by a degree or tertiary studies is in fact the first step in a life-long journey. The next step involves getting a job in your chosen profession.

Whose responsibility is it to equip under-graduates with the skills to acquire a job in their chosen employment? Is it the university's or is it the student's? The responsibility is ultimately the students to seek out these skills. Some tertiary institutions, which have the welfare and career interests of their students at heart, will encourage additional training or resources to assist prospective graduates' transition to employment.

One of the challenges students face when enrolling in a tertiary course is the expectation of a job and career as the ultimate outcome. Economic cycles, excessive student intakes, oversupply of some courses and the varying demands of potential employers are all key factors that affect employment opportunities; they directly affect potential new graduates' hopes for job and career opportunities.

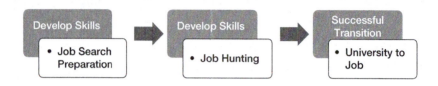

In the book, we will cover successful strategies for job search preparation and winning techniques for job hunting and securing a job. The focus of the book is on practical help, to assist you with achieving your personal plans for your transition to employment.

Despite our best intentions, after reading a valuable book or attending a worthwhile course we can fail to implement the things we have just learnt. This is often owing to the demands of busy lives and time pressures. For this reason, the material has been structured to allow students to progressively develop their personal plans. The book has been designed to be tailored to each student's personal needs (via the Personal Plan in the Appendix).

This introductory chapter will help you maximise your job search results. It will prepare you for the challenges and issues ahead. It teaches you to break a large task (job hunting) into smaller components and take one step at a time.

Chapter 2 on adaptable strategies will help you handle diminished work opportunities. It will outline alternate strategies to ensure your expectations are realistic and can match available job opportunities. You will learn ways to rebrand yourself and explore alternatives.

Chapter 3 on personal abilities explores ways of developing important personal skills for job hunting. These include adaptability, resilience, flexibility and endurance. The chapter provides encouragement.

Chapter 4, entitled Job hunting: key factors, will introduce you to the key considerations for job search preparation, including your achievements, job criteria, personal development, through to the role of a good resume and cover letter.

Chapter 5 is a key chapter, and will help you in locating job opportunities.

Social media is crucial in modern job searching. Four major platforms (LinkedIn, Facebook, Google Plus and Twitter) are covered in Chapters 6 to 8 to help you use these powerful options.

Good decision making is very important as you weigh up complex and often difficult options when undertaking job searching. Three decision-making tools are included to help you (Chapter 9). Through the Personal Plan you will identify your achievements. These are the "selling points" used in your job application (Chapters 10 and 11).

Progressively you will compile your Foundation Resume that contains all your achievements, qualifications, work experience and abilities (Chapters 12 and 13). It is a key resource for your job hunting. Resumes or CVs vary between countries and within regions. The book will outline the key differences (Chapter 15). This will help you select a format that is appropriate and culturally right. You will be guided through the creation of your job application Targeted Resume and cover letter.

Job interviews are a critical part of winning a job (Chapter 17). The key tips to succeed are included.

The Appendices: Resources provide valuable resources to assist your job search preparation.

The Appendices: Personal Plan is a key part. They help you convert the contents of the book into your personal action plan and produce key job application materials you will need.

eResources – the book's digital web resource – is a valuable source of digital resources to assist you.

1.2 Aims

Wisdom teaches us that if we do not have a travel plan we are unlikely to reach our destination. It is important to set goals – our aims.

This book aims to:

- equip prospective graduates with the skills to transition to successful employment;

- assist tertiary institutions to help their graduates into careers;
- allow the reader to develop their Personal Plans to win a job;
- explore Internet and social media techniques for job hunting, including LinkedIn, Facebook, Google Plus and Twitter; and
- provide added valuable digital resources via the book's eResource webpage.

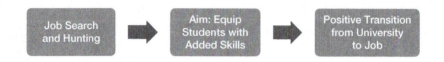

1.2.1 Structure

The book is organised to provide material in a structure that relates to the two main phases:

- job search preparation; and
- job hunting and securing a job.

The intent is to break the activity down into smaller, more manageable parts, to allow students to undertake the job preparation phase and then build on this for the job hunting and interview phases.

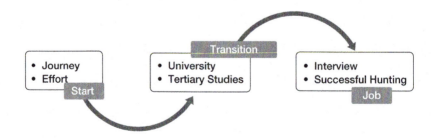

The graduate will learn:

- how the job market operates; and
- new skills and techniques to win a job.

1.2.2 Group discussion/tutorial

- Discuss the benefits of clearly setting your goals.
- What are the potential barriers or challenges to achieving these goals?

1.2.3 Personal Plan

There are two options for completing the Appendices: Personal Plan:

- hardcopy option in the back of the book; or
- digital Word option via the downloadable digital Appendices on the book's eResource website.

By completing the Appendices: Personal Plan digitally it will make it easy to edit it later across to your Foundation Resume and other job application documents.

This offers significant benefits. Progressively, for each chapter and its Personal Plan, you are building up valuable resource documents to help you with your job applications.

To download the eResource digital version of Appendices: Personal Plan, follow these instructions:

- Search: Routledge textbooks, or go to: www.routledge.com/
- Search window: type: "Your Career", which takes you to the eResources for this book.
- Alternatively, you can use the short cut: https://tinyurl.com/kyxnfaq
- Go to the Appendices <TAB> then click on the Personal Plan <TAB> (Appendices: Personal Plan) and follow the download instructions. You can then save the document to a working folder on your PC to create your own personal plan.

Now complete the relevant section in Appendix Personal Plan 1: Aims.

Complete your personal plan for:

- My priority goals.
- My short-term actions.
- My commitment.

1.3 Maximising your outcomes

We can read or listen, but are these the best ways to really learn? If we listen to information and follow up with discussion, this helps our understanding; it also helps relate the information to our particular situation. If we then complete an activity, this consolidates our learning. This book uses direct learning principles – you hear, you discuss, you do it yourself.

The Personal Plan involves your input. It means the course material is progressively converted to your needs. This maximises the potential outcomes of the course for you.

As you progressively work through the course material it is important to complete the Personal Plan sections. It provides key material for job applications.

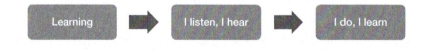

1.4 Challenges and issues

Wisdom teaches us: "If we do not know what we do not know, then we are in trouble. If we know what we do not know, then we can learn it."

The transition from university into employment and career is a move into unknown territory. It raises key questions: What job search preparation is required? How do I prepare a sound job application and resume? How do I go about locating potential jobs? How do I successfully complete the job selection interview?

Sometimes it is wise to understand the issues and challenges we face by viewing them from others' perspectives – that of the potential employer or interview panel.

| To know what you don't know | Is powerful | You can bridge the gap |

1.4.1 Challenges from under-graduate/graduate perspective

A question for the under-graduate/graduate might be:

- What are the added skills, resources and support I may need to transition to professional employment?

1.4.2 Challenges from an employer's perspective

Questions for a prospective employer might include:

- Can the prospective employee contribute to the goals and success of this organisation?
- Will they be a productive asset?
- How much additional training and development will they require to become productive members of the team?
- What is the potential of the prospective employee?

1.4.3 Challenges from the perspective of an interview panel

Challenges for the interview panel might include:

- Sorting through and evaluating many employment application letters. Which ones stand out? Which ones show potential? Which candidates should be interviewed?
- Evaluating resumes. Which stand out for interview? Which disclose skills and potential related to the job and the organisation?

1.4.4 Challenges from a university perspective

Questions for a university might include:

- What level of additional support and training do tertiary institutions provide to assist students into professional employment?
- What other resources can be provided for job search preparation and job hunting?

1.4.5 Group discussion/tutorial

- Discuss the new challenges and issues that stand out for you.
- Does looking at a challenge from the other side – employer or interview panel – help you understand? Can it help you?

1.4.6 Personal Plan

To download the eResource digital Appendices: Personal Plan, follow the instructions in the References at the end of the chapter.

Now complete Appendix Personal Plan 2: challenges and issues:

- My priority challenges.
- My priority actions.

Have you completed these sections of your Personal Plan? Then you may continue!

1.5 One step at a time

When we are facing a large activity or goal, it is understandable to feel somewhat overwhelmed. When we are moving into a whole new area such as searching for prospective employment, it can feel particularly daunting. These are both understandable and normal reactions.

Our first challenge is to get our thoughts and emotions under control. They can undermine what we want to do, if we let them. Once we get the processes right in our minds (and emotions) we feel good and we can then get working (our behaviour follows). A large activity or goal is just a combination of smaller project areas, which are in turn made up of lots of smaller tasks. By breaking them down, we can tackle big activities effectively.

First, see the big picture, the overall goal. Do not get caught up in the details of all the tasks immediately. It can make you feel overloaded and overwhelmed.

Secondly, identify the project areas to come – just the main themes – not the detailed tasks. Thirdly, focus on one specific task at a time.

This means our minds and emotions are not being distracted by other side tasks; these draw our focus away from our immediate task. Some people are multi-skilled and can do several tasks simultaneously, but in reality, their focus is skipping around. A clearer mind processes results if we have one task to work on. We devote all our abilities to it.

We can do this in the way we organise our work. For example, it is a good idea to have separate working folders or directories for each task or larger project area. Remove all other projects from your desk. Have just the immediate task material in front of you, ready to work on. Get organised. It helps focus you and your mind on the task at hand.

In his book, *Nine Things You Simply Must Do to Succeed in Love and Life*, Henry Cloud (2007) effectively addresses this issue. His advice is valuable. One of his principles is to continue to take small steps to victory. He refers to Isak Dinesen: "when you have a great and difficult task, something perhaps almost impossible, if you only work a little at a time, every day a little, suddenly the work will finish itself."

Sometimes, it is not any laziness on our part that hinders us, but the size of the activity ahead.

Cloud (2007) encourages us to learn from the ant:

- "Take the activity of any individual ant which seems to have little impact ... But the impact is happening and form is developing." It is the combined effort of small parts (or many ants) that achieves a lot.

- "I am concerned that until you begin to value the little steps and focus on them, not the big goal, you will always get discouraged and give up. Success will seem too slow to you."

- Whatever project you are undertaking, "it is done the same way: one brick at a time; one grain of sand at a time".

Small Steps Lead to Success

He reminds us of wise advice from Henry Ford (who developed the production of the world's first mass produced car, the Model T Ford) who said: "Nothing is particularly hard if you divide it into small jobs." He encourages us: "This principle enables those who have lost hope or are overwhelmed by the enormity of their problems to actually work their way to success."

1.5.1 Group discussion/tutorial

- What ways have you discovered to break up big jobs or big problems into parts we can handle?
- Does this make big projects and life easier?

1.5.2 Personal Plan

Now complete the relevant section in Appendix: Personal Plan 3: one step at a time. Identify a large project or activity that you face as you prepare for employment. Break it down into smaller tasks, which you can do.

So, now you have completed another section of your personal plan – one small section at a time, but progressively you are completing your job search Personal Plan.

1.6 Summary

In this introductory chapter, we have firstly explained the structure of this book. You will have recognised the importance of progressively completing the Personal Plan in the Appendix. This ensures you are not just reading a book, but step-by-step, you are applying what you have learnt. This will allow you to tailor the book to your personal needs.

This chapter has also covered clarifying aims and ways of maximising your outcomes in the job search process. It has identified some of the challenges and issues ahead so that you are prepared. The chapter emphasises breaking down a large task, such as job hunting, into smaller components and taking one step at a time.

In the following chapter, we will explore changing employment markets. We will help you adapt to the environment in which you are seeking a job. It may involve exploring or undertaking further studies.

At times, when there are few job opportunities in your preferred career area, we will help you look at alternative job options.

1.7 References and further reading

At the end of each chapter, we will provide you with key references for further reading. These will include textbooks on job hunting, websites with additional resources on specific aspects and some scholarly articles about the whole process of finding a job. These are mainly meant for university teachers seeking additional resources to assist their students in the teacher's field of education, to find suitable employment, as well as career advisors and employment professionals.

Cloud, H. (2007) *Nine Things You Simply Must Do to Succeed in Love and Life: A Psychologist Learns from His Patients What Really Works and What Doesn't.* (Thomas Nelson, Nashville, TN).

Peale, N.V. (2007) *The Power of Positive Thinking.* (Simon & Schuster, New York).

Schuller, R.H. (1986) *Move Ahead with Possibility Thinking*. (Jove Books, New York).

1.7.1   eResources link

To download the eResource digital version of Appendices: Personal Plan, follow these instructions:

- Search: Routledge textbooks, or go to: www.routledge.com/
- Search window: Type: "Your Career" which takes you to the eResources for this book.
- Alternatively, you can use the short cut: https://tinyurl.com/kyxnfaq
- Go to the Appendices <TAB> then click on the Personal Plan <TAB> (Appendices: Personal Plan) and follow the download instructions. You can then save the document to a working folder on your PC to create your own personal plan.

Adaptable strategies

2.1 Introduction

In this chapter we will explore ways to adapt to changing employment markets and job opportunities. We will help you recognise the value of having adaptable strategies.

It is important to review your expectations. Options such as further studies are discussed.

In cases of limited job opportunities in your chosen career or in your local area, options are explored for alternate careers and professions.

Rebranding yourself involves reviewing and re-presenting yourself. It recognises the wider aspects of your skills, education base and experiences. Often these can be used to help you rebrand yourself with skills and capabilities that fit other job options.

2.2 Adaptable alternate strategies: job searching

2.2.1 Adapting to changing employment markets

In the majority of cases for new graduates, there is a competitive market with many graduates applying for the same job. In the worst case scenarios, universities have produced an oversupply of graduates. The economy-business cycle may also be in recession. In this case, there may be little or no demand for new graduates.

How can a new graduate address this employment market situation? Clearly, they need to be trained to do this. This is the purpose of this book: to help new graduates to acquire job search skills, to be adaptable and to respond to changes in the employment marketplace.

There are several options graduates may need to explore if the job market is tight. These will increase your chances for employment. It is important to realistically recognise the actual employment market situation. This book can help you adapt your goals and expectations in terms of job opportunities.

2.2.1.1   Adaptable strategies

As with many aspects of life, it is valuable to have more than one strategy. If an archer has only one arrow in their quiver they are limited to one shot. Your aim is to have many arrows in your quiver; that is, to have many alternative options or different job search strategies.

There are several possible scenarios that you may face as you approach graduation:

- Positive local job market: opportunities will be available for new graduates in your profession in the locality in which you live.

- Poor local job market, but positive regional or interstate job market: opportunities for new graduates in your profession are available. However, they are further away and perhaps in the regional centre or different state or province. Perhaps opportunities in your specific field are even only available internationally.

2.2.1.2   Poor local job market: opportunities at different levels

If there are few opportunities at graduate level to meet your expectations, one option is to downsize your expectations. This involves widening your target to adjust to available jobs and the local market opportunities. Your choice, if living locally is important, may be to seek a lower-level entry job in your chosen profession. The strategy is to use this as a stepping stone. It will give you practical experience in an area of your chosen career. Significantly, it allows you to seek the graduate-level job you want at a later stage. It provides the security of job base from which you can further continue your search.

It also allows you to be seen by managers and supervisors. This is an opportunity for you to show that you can perform well at a lower-level role, are adaptable and would be suited to a graduate role.

2.2.2 *Expectations*

2.2.2.1 Realistic expectations

You will have acquired an awareness of the employment market you are about to enter. This is covered in Chapter 5 on locating job opportunities, which will help you understand the job market. Thus, you will be therefore able to modify your expectations so they are realistic. If they are excessive and out of touch with reality or the market, you will face disappointment.

Recognising market changes and adapting your approach to job hunting is a positive response to the real employment world you are about to enter.

2.2.2.2 Excessive expectations

Ideally, tertiary students will, after a lot of hard work, complete their course and be awarded a degree. In an ideal world, they would then move straight into a dream job – something they are trained for and interested in. In some cases this happens, but often it is not the norm. It can happen in some specialised careers where there is a shortage of professionals. Sometimes it is based on timing, for example, at a time when a graduate may be entering the job market during an economic business upturn and there is a demand for specific graduates and specialists.

It is important that the expectations of new graduates are realistic and not excessive. Adapting your expectations to the real world and the available job opportunities is sensible.

2.2.2.3   Re-orient job expectations

If there are few or no job opportunities (at graduate or lower entry-level) in your chosen profession, you may need to change. This will involve re-orienting your job expectations. You could take some of the key skills required in your course and use them for a different career option. For example, if you are a graduate civil engineer and there are few openings, you could explore opportunities for project team member in other or allied disciplines. While these may not be civil engineering roles, they would be using your skills. These may be roles that require problem solving, analysis or coordination skills for a multidisciplinary project.

In this case, assess the new market and opportunities. Modify and adapt your achievement statements, resume and job application. You are adapting to a changed employment marketplace. You are increasing your chances of a job.

2.2.3   Further studies

In the job searching and hunting phases you may have identified some barriers. It may be a shortage of employment opportunities for graduates. It may be the recognition that post-graduate qualifications or further studies are needed. This may reflect a difference between what employers are seeking and those skills provided through an under-graduate course.

After many years of study, the thought of further study may seem daunting. It may be something to evaluate. Use the decision-making tools outlined in Chapter 9 of this book. These tools will help you analyse complex situations and make choices. They include: decision support, SWOT analysis (strengths, weaknesses, opportunities and threats) and force field analysis.

These tools can assist you to assess different options including job search level, area of search and short-term personal goals. The process you go through will help you clarify your thinking and your decisions.

Digital versions of the decision-making tools are available through the eResources (see the decision tools <TAB>).

2.2.4 *Alternative career or profession*

One of the greatest challenges an under-graduate faces when choosing a degree course is "Have I selected the right course for my future career?" Nowadays, it is unfortunate that there seems to be less attention paid to vocational assessment prior to entry into a tertiary course. These evaluations may include a Myers-Briggs Type Indicator® (MBTI)®, a Strong Interest Inventory (SII) or other evaluations. They are briefly outlined in Chapter 9: Personal development (see Section 9.2: Understanding yourself). They may be useful to you if they help you evaluate alternative career and personal choices. In particular, they may assist you to see if a job or career fits your personality or your characteristics. There are online career assessment services. These link your assessment and personal characteristics to the common characteristics of different jobs.

For example, some have linked MBTI® and SII assessments to a large US database of different jobs and professions, along with their characteristics. They provide an analysis and report on you and your characteristics in relation to particular careers. The report provides guidance on careers and jobs that seem to match your characteristics.

Further aspects of online career assessments are covered in more detail later in Chapter 9: Personal development, as well as in Appendix Resources 1: Myers-Briggs Type Indicator® (MBTI®) and Appendix Resources 2: Career assessment reports.

2.2.4.1   Reference: example sites for career assessment

CPP (USA) (The People Development People): www.cpp.com

OPP (Europe) (CPP in Europe): www.opp.com

Career Assessment Site: www.careerassessmentsite.com

Direct digital links to these sites are available via the eResources website.

To access the eResources, go to the eResources link in the References at the end of this chapter.

After doing such an evaluation and self-assessment, you may consider an alternative career path. This may initially seem hard and you may fear that you have lost benefits from courses that you have completed. A closer analysis may show that there could be positives. The courses and subjects you completed provide you with skills and abilities that you may carry over into other areas. To be happy in your job and career is important. Making a decision to change may in fact be a positive change for your life. This approach will require you to be adaptable, recognise the skills required and build a new career strategy. This is about adapting and making new career choices that will ultimately benefit you. The courses and modules that you have completed may have provided a strong base for further studies towards new career directions.

2.2.5   Recognising your skills and using them

It is important to recognise that the degree you have completed is not wasted if you choose to change. You have acquired a wide range of skills through undertaking your tertiary studies. These are abilities that you can carry forward into a new career.

Tertiary studies can provide:

- Specialist knowledge and training (particularly for vocationally-oriented courses).

- General skills: analysis, research, problem solving, meeting deadlines, writing and communication, and computer skills (Word, spreadsheets and so on), etc.

The latter general skill sets apply across many jobs and professions. These are detailed in Chapters 10 and 11 on General Achievements and Achievements: Extended.

Your general skills will be identified as you complete the Personal Plan appendices for Chapters 10 and 11 (Appendices Personal Plan 10 and 11).

From these you will have recognised your wider achievements and skills; they are often common to many graduate jobs. Your efforts in undertaking a degree course have provided you with skill sets that you can adapt to different career paths.

2.3 Rebranding yourself

There is a saying that "a leopard can't change its spots". Is this about its outward appearance or its internal characteristics? The real characteristics of a leopard are not so much its outward appearance but its other inner abilities such as endurance and hunting skills.

When you present yourself for a job, you are presenting your outer achievements as well as your inner characteristics and abilities. Sometimes, these need to be fine-tuned, rebranded or highlighted to relate to the new position. We will show you ways to present yourself – rebrand your appearance – as it relates to new jobs.

How we present or brand ourselves depends on how we see ourselves. It also depends on our personal presentation skills. These can be developed and this book will help you understand these.

Our personal branding comes from our experiences, skills, abilities and training. It comes from our background. It also comes from how we view ourselves. By taking a wider view of yourself, you will recognise other abilities and skills you possess. This could be from other areas where you have developed skills – life activities or hobbies, part-time work, a role in a sporting organisation or church, or volunteer activities. These all provide achievements that will add to your job application and resume.

Rebrand Yourself

The same experience or achievements can be presented in widely different ways. One presentation may focus on the original activity or organisation, whereas the other presentation option focuses on the underlying skills that have been developed and relates them to a new organisation or job. Both presentations are correct but have different impacts and aims. One relates to your role in another external organisation; the other relates the skills you have developed to the new position; that is, the job you are seeking.

Your challenge is to draw the link between the skills in the previous role and the skills for the position for which you are applying. You should aim to make the link to a potential new job easy for the interview panel to recognise. Do not just hope that they can work out if there is a connection.

A young graduate may have had an earlier work experience before undertaking a different course. Is that prior experience relevant to a new job in a different professional area? Can they be linked? The answer is often yes. The way to go about it is the way you brand yourself.

For example, a young graduate may have had an earlier work experience as a cartographer or mapmaker before undertaking a different course. The skills gained in this earlier role could be presented in technical map-making or cartography terms. The skills may appear to have little relation to another new job. Alternatively, you can brand it in terms of your new job. The wrong way would be to express the teamwork experience as: "I was a member of a multidisciplinary cartographic team. It involved integrating geographic systems and close teamwork between different spatial information specialists." This makes it hard to relate this past experience to a new and different job role.

A better and more general way would be to express the same skill differently: "In an earlier role I was a member of a multidisciplinary team. It involved close teamwork to create cooperation and team culture. My skills in team building were well developed."

This is rebranding yourself. The technical cartography or map-making terms are removed. The focus switches to the teamwork aspect, which is the key part of most jobs and can easily be related to the job criteria of another new position.

| Recognise your achievements | → | Remove unrelated aspects | → | Rebrand your achievements |

There are several reasons to rebrand ourselves:

- Build on and recognise past achievements.
- Relate our past experiences and achievements to the new job criteria.
- Make it easy for prospective employees to recognise our achievements and experience.
- Gain a different view of our abilities.
- Learn to present ourselves (in job application and interview) in a different way that relates to the new job.

You are not changing your "leopard spots", but expressing them in a different way – as abilities and achievements that are easily related to a new job.

In Chapter 10: General Achievements and Chapter 11: Achievements: extended you will identify your skills and develop your personal achievement statements; these are important as they can assist you in rebranding yourself.

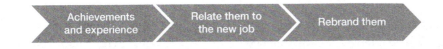

| Achievements and experience | Relate them to the new job | Rebrand them |

Your rebranding may be due to:

- Past experiences and achievements that you wish to cross-relate to a potential new job criteria.
- Changes in job opportunities, where you have decided to take a different job path, but remain in the same career area.

Changes?

2.3.1 Job market changes and alternative job options

There may be changes to the job market. In this case, you may decide to seek a different job or career option. This may be allied to your degree, but in a different career area. This shows flexibility and an ability to react to changes in the job market and changing job opportunities available.

2.3.2 Personal preference changes

As you undertake a university degree or tertiary qualification, your areas of interest can change. This may be to an interest in a particular sector of your chosen profession. For example, from early childhood development, moving towards a more specialised area such as childhood disorders; or from general nursing to a specialisation such as midwifery. It is wonderful if your changing interests can be matched to your new employment opportunities in your chosen specialisation. This may involve added study units.

If the choice is right for you, you may need to rebrand yourself. You could rebrand subjects you have completed to show their links to a different but allied career area.

2.4 Summary

In a changing world with changing job opportunities, this chapter has identified adaptable alternate strategies to match available job openings. These could include further studies or different career options.

This chapter has also outlined ways to rebrand yourself and explore positive job alternatives.

In the next chapter we will look at the importance of personal factors in job searching. It will outline ways to encourage you to be adaptable, resilient and have endurance in your job search. Different techniques will be outlined and key considerations in the job search process will be explored.

2.5 References and further reading

Arruda, W. and Dixson, K. (2007) *Career Distinction: Stand Out by Building Your Brand*. (Wiley, Hoboken, NJ, USA).

Miedaner, T. (2010) *Coach Yourself to a New Career: 7 Steps to Reinventing Your Professional Life*. (McGraw-Hill, New York, NY, USA).

Myers-Briggs Type Indicator® (MBTI)®. Developed by Katherine Cook Briggs and Isabel Briggs Myers.

Myers & Briggs Foundation, available at: www.myersbriggs.org

Pollak, L. (2012) *Getting from College to Career: Your Essential Guide to Succeeding in the Real World*. (Harper Business, New York, NY, USA, rev. edn).

Sweeny, J. (2014) *Moving the Needle: Get Clear, Get Free and Get Going in Your Career, Business and Life!* (Wiley, Hoboken, NJ, USA).

2.5.1 Some reference websites for career assessment

Career Assessment Site, available at: www.careerassessmentsite.com

CPP (USA): The People Development People, available at: www.cpp.com

OPP (Europe) (CPP in Europe), available at: www.opp.com

2.5.2 Reference: eResources link for this book

For added resources and digital files related to this chapter.

Search: Routledge Text Books or go to: www.routledge.com/

Search Window: Type "Your Career" which will take you to the eResources for this book.

Or via the short cut: https://tinyurl.com/kyxnfaq

Then go to the Web References <TAB> and then the References <TAB>.

3 Personal abilities

3.1 Introduction

This chapter will help your recognise the importance of personal factors in the job search process. You will be encouraged to build adaptability, resilience and endurance.

It is important that you can encourage yourself and overcome rejections. Techniques for uplifting your spirit are discussed. The value of family, mentors and friends in providing support are outlined. You will be encouraged to tap into sources of external support to help and encourage you in your job search.

3.2 Developing personal abilities for successful job hunting

This book will assist you with developing skills to research jobs, hunt jobs and win them. What other qualities and skills will you need to make a positive transition from tertiary studies to employment? This is crucial information. If you know the abilities that you will need, you can take steps to acquire them. If you do not know what is required, you may be floating along and just hoping for the best.

Developing the personal abilities for job hunting is important. Sometimes it can be tough and challenging. Sometimes it can be spiritually and mentally draining. It is important to develop techniques to lift your spirit and keep encouraging yourself.

Why is this so often overlooked when training young people for careers and even life?

Researching, planning and job hunting can be a significant challenge. What other personal skills will you need to handle this challenge? These same skills will be a valuable asset through life. They can assist you in your career and life journey.

Let us identify these extra personal skills; they include adaptability, resilience and endurance. Explore these topics: check what is on the web, read about them, practise them and do courses to strengthen your abilities. They will help you get through the tough times, disappointments and workloads associated with finding a new job.

- *Adaptability*: this is the ability to change and accommodate changing circumstances (the chameleon characteristic).

- *Resilience*: this is the ability to bounce back after setbacks or disappointments (the rubber ball characteristic).

- *Endurance*: this is the ability to keep going (marathon characteristic). It is about recognising that the job hunt is often more a marathon than a sprint.

This book is about being prepared and building techniques for successful job hunting. While these personal development aspects are outside the scope of this book, they are abilities we would encourage you to develop further. It will be a great investment in your personal development, your career advancement and life journey.

Recognise these personal aspects and their value. Invest time and effort into building your abilities in these areas.

The challenges ahead may require all your effort, commitment, endurance and even adaptability. Keeping your outlook positive and your thoughts uplifted is important. Maintaining positive mind patterns is important. At other times, you will need courage and inner resources to draw on. Quite often, finding a job can be difficult and even disheartening. It can test your self-belief, stamina and coping strategies.

As literature that provides wisdom (e.g. includes the Bible as one example) teaches us, it is sometimes in the seemingly harder parts of life's journey that we build the greatest strengths. When you recognise that job searching is hard and that it will require significant effort, you can rise to the challenge. At times, when job markets are difficult or opportunities are few, you will need encouragement to keep going.

3.2.1 Adaptability

Adaptability is the ability to change to meet changing circumstances. In a rapidly changing world it is a valuable trait to develop. For some people, it comes naturally; for others, they may need to work to develop it. The changes in types of employment and the rate of change are increasing. Experts suggest that the next major group of jobs have not yet have come into existence.

Economies change, employment markets change and skill requirements from employers change. It has been suggested that many in today's generation will, on average, have six or more careers in their lifetime. That is not just different jobs, but different roles and careers. This will require adaptability to handle the change.

Adaptability

Some people require and prefer familiarity. For many, sameness, as opposed to change, provides comfort. They enjoy going to the same place for a holiday. For other people, they need change to feel stimulated. For them, sameness equates to boredom. They enjoy change and adapting. Forty years of working in the same field, for the same employer – those days are over for most professions.

Explore books, online courses and ways you can build adaptability. It can be a valuable asset in getting your first job, and also in your life and career.

3.2.2 Resilience

Resilience is the ability to cope with challenges and bounce back. It is the ability to surmount difficulties. Some people just have it, others need to learn it. Unless you are exceedingly lucky, you will need resilience at some points in your life.

Resilience

One of the great development challenges for young people is building resilience. That includes allowing them to fail at times and then grow through it. Overly protective parenting can unwittingly hinder the development of this life skill. Young adults need to learn this ability and build resilience if they are to cope with life and its challenges. Look for ways to build this life skill. Treat setbacks as an opportunity to learn and to bounce back.

3.2.3 Endurance

Endurance is the ability to keep going and to last the distance. Sometimes job hunting may seem like a marathon. Just as marathon runners train to build endurance, you can build the ability to last. Job hunting can require physical stamina; doing a lot of work in preparing for the job search through to the actual job hunt. The whole process will take time and effort, so you will need endurance.

Endurance

Endurance can be both mental and spiritual; your mind controls your behaviour and feelings. Your inner spiritual being also controls your feelings and actions. If you are going through a difficult period and feel you will not make it, then it is time to work on your thought patterns. Build up techniques for positive thinking. Those with spiritual beliefs can draw on their faith, spiritual encouragement or literature that provides wisdom. This can encourage and assist you to last the distance when the going seems tough.

It is important to share your concerns with others if you feel your endurance is wavering. A problem shared is a problem halved. Just speaking about an issue of concern allows your subconscious to begin working on solutions or even provide a clearer perspective.

The process of preparing your job search and undertaking the job hunt will require endurance. Realise that you have already shown endurance as you complete your tertiary studies. This will give you added encouragement that you have endurance.

3.2.4 Spirit lifters and thought conditioners

3.2.4.1 Spirit lifters

These are positive affirmations that can lift our souls when we are feeling overburdened. The positive words can sooth us and encourage us. At times, life's challenges can appear to be a battlefield of the mind. The small negative inner voice that sows doubts can be troubling. As you learn to recognise it and respond with positive affirmations you can move from the negative to the positive. Spiritual material and literature that provides wisdom can be powerful. They can equip us to handle the challenges of life. By lifting our spirits, we can lift our behaviour and our feelings to meet problems or disappointments and overcome them.

Search for, and build a collection of spirit lifters. Different faiths have words of wisdom and encouragement. The Bible has many. Learn positive affirmations and verses (spirit lifters) that will encourage you. Say them out loud to yourself. Practice ways to lift your spirit.

Use Spirit Lifters

3.2.4.2 Thought conditioners

Just as we can do gym work to develop our bodies, using thought conditioners works on a similar principle for our thought patterns. They can help people build up their spirit and their souls. Negative thought patterns can overwhelm us or make us less able to function. Thought conditioners can help overcome negative thought patterns that can drag us down.

They can help us develop positive thought patterns. Look out for thought conditioners and verses to encourage you. There are books on positive thinking; for example those of Robert Schuller and Norman Vincent Peale. Literature that provides wisdom and spiritual literature have words of wisdom to encourage us. These can speak into our minds and our souls. Learn several positive thought conditioners and practice using them; for example, "I will persevere and will find the right job". They can be a remarkable asset during tough periods of job searching. You can also use them through life.

Our thoughts control our feelings and our behaviour (our responses). A framework that encourages positive responses to challenges will help us overcome difficulties. It is a valuable technique for life.

3.2.5 Mentors, friends and family support

3.2.5.1 Mentors

These can be a valuable asset. They can listen and provide guidance. They can also make you realise you are not alone in the challenges that you are facing. They can be a wonderful source of support when job hunting becomes tough.

Family, Friends & Mentors Can Help

3.2.5.2 Family and friends

These are people who you can call on to provide support and encouragement. They do not need to have detailed knowledge of your career area. A supportive friend or family member and a listening ear can do wonders. Just by sharing your worries with a family member or friend, is like sharing the burden. Via your sharing, you can build trust with your friend and they can provide support in times of tough challenges.

Job hunting can be a tough phase. At times, it may seem impossible to stay positive and realise that your efforts will eventually pay off. The support of a family member or friend can help you. It can help lift burdens you are carrying and restore your enthusiasm and energy.

Call on Family & Friends → Share Burdens → Take in their support

3.3 Summary

In this chapter we have explored the value of building personal attributes such as adaptability, resilience and endurance. Techniques to encourage you and lift your spirits have been introduced. These will help you through tough times and possible rejections in your job search. The aim is to keep trying. You will succeed as you adapt to the opportunities available.

In the following chapter we will explore the key factors in job hunting, including: why people win jobs; adapting to change; resumes and cover letters; social media in job searching; and your online image.

3.4 References and further reading

3.4.1 Further reading

Peale, N.V. (2003) *The Power of Positive Thinking* (Simon and Schuster, New York, NY, USA). Extensive range of books.

Schuller, R.H. (1967–1984) *Possibility Thinking* (Penguin Random House, New York, NY, USA). Extensive range of books.

3.4.2 General books on finding a job

Bolles, R.N. (2016) *What Color Is Your Parachute?: A Practical Manual for Job-Hunters and Career-Changers* (Penguin Random House, New York, NY, USA).

Cannon, J. (2009) *Finding a Job: 7 Steps to Success* (Cannon Career Development, Inc. Boston, MA, USA).

Levinson, J.C. and Perry, D. (2011) *Guerrilla Marketing for Job Hunters 3.0* (Wiley, Hoboken, NJ, USA).

Tieger, P.D. and Barron, B. (2011) *Do What You Are: Discover the Perfect Career for You Through the Secrets of Personality Type* (Scribe, Brunswick, Victoria, Australia).

3.4.3 Scholarly articles

Campbell, M. (2008) Local policies to beat long-term unemployment. (*Local Government Studies*, Vol. 19, Issue 4, pp. 505–518).

Owens, W.T. (2012) Surviving a job search in Teacher education: An applicant's perspective and critique. (*Action in Teacher Education*, Vol. 21, Issue 3, pp. 79–87).

4 | Job hunting
Key factors

4.1 Introduction

In this chapter we will explore key factors in job hunting. These include: the importance of a good resume and cover letter; the psychology behind job selection and how to use it; and the key role of social media in job searching. The importance of reviewing your online image is also outlined.

Job Hunting

4.2 Overview of job hunting and securing a job

What are the techniques and considerations required to win the job? If you can master these then you are heading in the right direction to start your new employment.

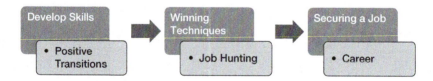

These will be developed later in Chapters 10 and 11 and they will form the basis for your Foundation Resume.

4.2.1 Achievements and job criteria: overview

Job criteria indicate the experience, skills and characteristics required for a position. What are your achievements in these areas? The common ones include: teamwork, communication, commitment, people skills, quality, timeliness and customer service.

Later in the book you will see how to recognise your achievements and how to create your personal achievements statements. These will become valuable resources for your resume, job application and interview preparation.

Recognise Your Achievements

4.2.2 Good resume

Transforming your education, training, experience, skills, personal values and achievements into a good resume is an art. It requires the investment of time and effort. It is a great investment in the preparation phase for a new job. This book will outline the key elements of a good resume. Your aim is to present yourself in a way so your achievements and abilities stand out.

Good Resume
Job Application Cover Letter

4.2.3 Cover letter: overview

The book will take you through the key parts of the cover letter for job applications. A well written cover letter linking to the key job criteria enhances your chances.

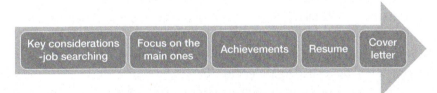

4.3 Job hunting: key considerations

4.3.1 Why do some people win jobs and others not?

There are some common aspects regarding winning a job. It is not just about the person with the highest qualifications or highest grade point average. Surprisingly, it is about other factors. It is about the psychology of why people are selected. We will help you to understand and use these techniques. It is about understanding job selection from the employer's perspective. The aim is to help the manager achieve their goals and at the same time meet your goal of winning a new position. This is covered in more detail in a following section on "Job selection: psychology".

4.3.2   Adapting to change

We are in a rapidly changing world. Some people struggle with this and are averse to change – they prefer the familiar. Others love change and thrive on it. They dislike routine and lack of variety.

The ability to change yourself or adapt to changing circumstances such as a changing job market is a valuable trait. For those who have it already and are adaptable, the book will help you use these skills in your job search. For those who do not have change and adaptation traits, this book will encourage you to develop them and will explain the benefits in your job searching.

4.3.3   Value and power of a good resume

The book will give you the skills and understanding to prepare a Foundation Resume. It is intended as your resource that contains your abilities, qualifications and experience. A Targeted Resume will follow on later. It will use a resume layout that you will select for your target country and region. It will be related to a specific job.

The challenge is to write well and present yourself professionally. Your resume possibly will be competing with many others. Your aim is to present yourself in a way so your achievements and abilities stand out.

Value and Power of a Good Resume

The test is whether a person evaluating your application and resume can quickly and easily see who you are. It should highlight your abilities and achievements; in particular it should relate them to the job criteria. The aim is to match your abilities to the job criteria. If your resume is good in relation to the job criteria, you will increase your chances of selection for an interview; if not, your application may be rejected.

Positive Impact of a Good Cover Letter

4.3.4   Value of a good cover letter

A well written cover letter will allow the person assessing application to immediately see that you match the key job criteria; it leads you towards an interview. In some cases applicants can be rejected on the basis of the cover letter. Poorly written cover letters or ones that do not address the job clearly can lead to rejection even before your resume is read.

4.3.5   Researching potential employment organisations

It is a valuable investment of your time to research any organisation to which you are applying. Look for wider details about its goals and main activities. This greater understanding can carry through to added parts in your application, cover letter or resume; it may provide links between yourself and the new job or organisation.

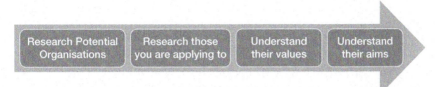

It will be potentially useful in a job interview if wider questions arise about the organisation or the job. It will show that you are thorough in your preparation and that you do your homework. These are valuable positive traits when evaluating potential employees.

35

4.3.6 Social media for job searching

Social media such as LinkedIn, Facebook, Google Plus and Twitter are becoming key online ways for employers to advertise and fill new positions. Likewise, they are becoming the key ways for those seeking jobs.

Social Media for Job Searching

Job hunting today has moved from newspapers and online job boards searching to social media. These platforms allow job seekers to connect with and attract potential employers. Employers also use social media to find qualified applicants. It is a fast and inexpensive way to find good job candidates.

LinkedIn is a number one social network for job searching. If you only have time for one social network for job searching, then LinkedIn may be the one you should use. Indeed is another key online job search site in many countries. There are others in different countries and regions. Check your area to identify the major job searching network and link into it. Social networks are increasingly being used by recruiters and employers.

LinkedIn continues to dominate, but Facebook, Google Plus and Twitter each offer capabilities to support job searching and an online professional presence (bio-profile) plus links to job opportunities.

Using social media to locate potential job opportunities is increasingly important and even crucial. You want every advantage you can gain. You need to understand the main social media for job hunting: that is, LinkedIn, Facebook, Google Plus and Twitter. It will help you choose the most appropriate one(s) for your job hunting.

Social media offer the potential to identify new jobs and apply for them online. The opportunities to successfully gain a new job will be increased.

4.3.7 Checking yourself: your online image

As well as you researching and checking out the organisation, they will possibly check you out before offering an interview. Think about the following questions:

- How will you appear if they Googled your name?
- How will you come across in your social media pages (such as Facebook)?

Is this the person you want a potential employer to see? Will they recognise positive values and valuable personal aspects? Will they see things they may not prefer to have as an employee or part of their organisation?

4.3.7.1   Social media: the real you?

Investing time in reviewing the way you project yourself via social media is valuable. If this is not the personal image you wish to project to a potential employer, then action is needed. Explore ways to clean it, amend and improve it. It may be the difference between a job offer or rejection.

Unfortunately we cannot erase all our online history. But there are ways you can improve and fix up your social media presentation as you move forward into job applications.

You want to show a potential employer the real you – your positive abilities, capabilities and achievements. Images of you having fun and enjoying life are fine, but if it involves inappropriate pictures and lifestyles, you are not presenting yourself well.

Work out what changes are needed and start to make them. The aim is to present the best side of yourself, not your weaknesses or possibly poor aspects. Consider restricting access to your social media pages via the privacy settings.

4.3.8   *Professional development: overview*

For some, professional development follows only after you have a job; however, you can commence professional development prior to getting a job.

If possible, consider using your time, before you apply for a job, to undertake professional development. This is a valuable investment. It will show potential employers that you are committed to your chosen profession and have initiative to develop yourself. Areas to investigate where you can possibly develop yourself are:

- Professional bodies: apply and join up as an under-graduate or graduate member.

- Seek their advice.
- Ask them for opportunities to link with a mentor to guide you.
- Do a short course.
- Read a book.
- Do an online course.

Start Your Professional Development

Any professional development you undertake after graduation will assist you. It helps your personal and professional growth, and it helps your job application. It will show potential employers that you are investing in your professional development and that you recognise its value. This is a characteristic that employers value in a potential employee. Keep growing and developing personally.

4.4 Job selection: psychology

The first thing to recognise is that your job hunting takes place in a competitive market. You need to ensure your application (cover letter, resume and interview) makes you stand out as the best candidate.

The second is to recognise the process from the viewpoint of the manager or interview panel. These are busy people and the interview selection process is an added load. Your aim should be to make their job easy. A well written application that shows links to the job criteria helps them to do the evaluation.

The third is understanding the psychology of why managers employ a particular person for a vacancy. What motivates them or influences their decision? Is it the highest qualifications? The best experience? Or, the person with people skills who can present themselves well?

Of course there are a number of factors and those above are just some of them. We want you to understand all these factors so you can use them to help you in applying for a job.

Understand Job Selection Psychology

There is a deeper psychological reason why a manager employs a person. It is based on the following key questions: will the potential employee help the manager to:

- do his or her work better;

- support the manager's goals (these may be personal goals or work dictated performance indicators);

- make the organisation or business successful; and

- overcome problems and challenges the manager is facing.

How can you respond to these deeper psychological motivations? It can be easily done by preparing (in writing) and practising short "helping statements" that respond to these needs.

These short statements can be selectively added to your interview responses. In response to a question about your qualifications you can reply by listing them.

Alternatively, you can list them in your response and add a helping statement at the end; for example, "my qualifications are (...), which I believe will help you manage (activity)".

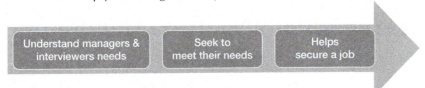

Understand managers & interviewers needs → Seek to meet their needs → Helps secure a job

4.4.1 Group discussion/tutorial

- Discuss the importance of the issue of meeting the manager's needs.

- How important are these in the overall selection? What is your opinion?

4.4.2 Personal Plan

To download the eResource digital Appendices: Personal Plan, follow the instructions in the References at the end of the chapter.

Now complete Appendix: Personal Plan 4: job selection psychology and create your added "helping statements".

4.5 Understanding the job market

Researching the market that you are trying to enter is valuable. If you know the potential job market, you can adapt your strategy and optimise your chances of winning a job.

Assess the job market for your chosen career – locally, regionally and interstate. What is the job market like in careers allied to your degree area?

Sources can include:

- National employment data (national or state bureaux of statistics – surveys and reports).

- National or state employment agencies (seek surveys by broad employment sector (e.g. health) or professional sector, such as physiotherapists).

- State employment data – check government websites for periodic surveys of employment by sector.

- Online job agencies where you can search for vacancies for a profession by geographical region.

Research and Understand the Job Market

Consult with a professional institution that covers your career area. If you are not an associate member, consider joining to assist your professional development.

Key questions to ask include:

- What is the job market like for graduates in (specific area)? (e.g. civil engineering).

- What is the employment market like in other regions or states?

- What associated career areas might offer stronger prospects for a graduate in (specific area)?

As you research and compile this information, it will give you a deeper understanding of employment opportunities. It will help you plan your job search strategy.

4.5.1 Job lists

These are a consolidation of advertised vacancies and opportunities. It means you can find details of a particular career and job openings on a consolidated website.

Job search companies that have a well-developed online presence or website will do the same.

Some specialise in different sectors of the employment market. Do a web search and research the best ones for your region and job type. Use them to track job opportunities. Those that allow you to submit your job search profile and keywords, and who will then advise you when openings come up, are particularly valuable.

You can specify job title, keywords or company. In addition enter city, state or postcode. Click "find jobs" to get a listing of jobs that meet these criteria. They can save a lot of time and make job searching easier.

See www.indeed.com/job in the References at the end of this chapter.

4.5.2 Social media: job market

Career Profiles (a US career and job search company) advises on the importance of social network sites when looking for a job. The US Bureau of Labor Statistics reports that 70% of all jobs are found through networking. "There are a number of online resources designed just for this purpose, and learning to use them effectively will put you at a real advantage in today's competitive job market." See Career Profiles, www.careerprofiles.info, in the References at the end of this chapter.

Social media that reflect job openings and opportunities can be a valuable source of information on the job market in your profession or career area.

LinkedIn is the principal professional and career-related social media site in many countries.

Others include Facebook Careers, Google Plus and Twitter.

Use LinkedIn (and others) as a reference source to assess opportunities and job openings in your preferred career or profession. Check out opportunities for related jobs to your preferred graduate position if the job market is poor in your chosen career area or locality.

Use the advertised positions to assess the job market. Use it as a guide as you prepare for job hunting. By understanding the job market you can adapt your job search strategy and approach.

Social Media: Valuable for Job Searching

In Chapters 6 to 8 on social media for job searching, this topic will be covered in more detail.

See LinkedIn, Job Search: www.linkedin.com in the References at the end of this chapter.

4.6 Summary

In this chapter you have identified some of the key factors for job hunting. This chapter has been provided to let you understand the stages ahead. Section 4.4 Job selection: psychology will have provided some further understanding of the question: "Why do some people win jobs?"

Understanding and using "helping statements" that tap into the psychology of job selection, will assist you.

An overview of the job market you are seeking to enter has been provided. An introduction to social media for job searching has been done and it will be covered in more detail in later chapters.

In the next chapter, the key area of locating job opportunities will be covered. This includes traditional approaches, job search agencies, support services, online techniques through to social media for job searching.

4.7 References and further reading

Career Profiles. *Job Searching Social Networking Sites*. www.careerprofiles.info

Indeed.com/job search: Job Search. www.indeed.com/jobs

LinkedIn. Job Search. www.linkedin.com

4.7.1 Reference: eResources link for this book

For added resources and digital files related to this chapter:

Search/go to: Routledge Text Books or www.routledge.com/

Search window: type "Your Career"; it will then take you to the eResources for this book.

Or you can access the eResources via the short cut: https://tinyurl.com/kyxnfaq

Then go to the Appendices <TAB>, Personal Plan <TAB> (Appendices: Personal Plan) and follow the download instructions. Then save it to a working folder on your PC.

The above references are available via clickable links on the eResource website.

Go to the Web References <TAB> then the References <TAB> and follow the link.

5 Locating job opportunities

5.1 Introduction

This chapter will cover the different ways to locate job opportunities. It covers the following: an overview of options; understanding traditional job processes; the hidden job market; and social media job markets and online Internet opportunities. It provides an outline of the main types of job search agencies and how they can assist.

It introduces non-advertised jobs and how to link to them and networking to increase job opportunities.

As part of your Personal Plan you will identify job search areas to focus on and types of organisations to contact. It will include a plan on which social media platforms you may link into for job searching.

5.2 Locating job opportunities

Locating Job Opportunities

5.2.1 Job location: overview

The first key step to winning employment is locating job opportunities. If you miss a job opening you have no chance of getting the job. Your chances improve when you understand how the job system works, how it varies and which avenues to follow. The more avenues you are searching and exploring, the more chances you will have. If one graduate has used the techniques in this book they may perhaps identify 20% more job opportunities. They will then have an advantage over other job search graduates. Their chances will increase by 20% for this factor alone.

44

The aims of this chapter are to increase your chances of locating job opportunities. This increases your chances of winning a job.

5.2.1.1   Locating jobs: options

- Understanding the job market: traditional.
- Hidden job market.
- Social media: locating job opportunities.
- Advertisements: press.
- Online Internet opportunities.
- Job search agencies (servicing employers).
- Job search agencies (servicing potential employees): government.
- Non-advertised jobs.
- Networking: job opportunities.
- Networking: approaching organisations.

5.2.1.2   Group discussion/tutorial

Discuss: how would you rate your skills, knowledge or understanding of how the job market works (in areas such as locating job opportunities, techniques for locating jobs, using agencies, using online techniques or websites, networking or internal hidden job markets).

I would rate my current skills/knowledge as:

Nil   Limited   Low   Moderate   High

Discuss: your priority areas to work on.

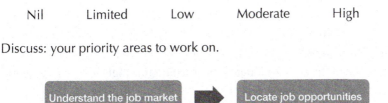

5.2.2   *Understanding the traditional job market*

The traditional method of filling a job vacancy is via newspaper advertisements. For smaller private organisations, this involves a manager preparing the job criteria and job advertisement, then responding to applications, shortlisting those to interview and running the interview process. It is quite a load on top of the manager's normal workload.

For larger private organisations or the government sector, this process will involve shared responsibilities. This could be between the manager and the human resources department (or personnel section). Again, this involves an added load on the manager's time. An alternative approach involves engaging an employment (job search) agency. They are contracted to take on the majority of the work to advertise, interview and select potential employees (either one final candidate or a shortlist of perhaps three for the manager to assess and interview). This approach uses professional job searchers and human resource specialists. While they can lack the intimate knowledge of the technical professional work area, they can bring additional human relations skills.

5.2.3   Hidden job market

Employers may locate suitable candidates from social media and professional career sites such as LinkedIn and the profiles of job seekers. The job does not need to be advertised, as suitable candidates can be assessed, interviewed and selected from their online profiles. They can be identified from their online profiles and bio information (equivalent to an online resume), which is listed on a social media site that supports job searching (examples include LinkedIn, Facebook, Google Plus and Twitter). Therefore, ensuring you have a professional presence and a job search bio (biography) on social media job sites is important.

There is another hidden job market. These are jobs you find out from network contacts. They may be advertised internally or filled via recommendations from another professional within the organisation or external to it. They are not advertised, but just filled. This is more likely for advanced positions rather than for graduate positions. Increasingly, this is happening via social media and job websites.

Another option for job seekers is to develop contacts within several job search agencies. Their role is to find someone to fill the job vacancies. If you and your resume are already on their books, you have a head start and an improved chance.

Some agencies work for and represent employers, businesses and other organisations that are seeking to fill a vacancy. Some other agencies represent employees who are seeking a job. Their role and function is to represent you and help you find employment.

There is another job market sector you need to understand and use to your advantage. These can include state or national government agencies (or subcontracting organisations) who offer free employment services. As in most cases, you will be new to job searching in your career area so a smart strategy is to seek advice from experts in this sector.

People can value being asked for their professional advice. This type of request could include professionals or managers in your chosen career area; it should include job search professionals as well. Together, both of these areas can provide you with complementary valuable advice. One is a perspective from the profession or manager, the other the perspective of a job search professional. Online social media platforms such as LinkedIn can help you network, to build contacts in your prospective career area and to seek advice from professionals via online links.

5.2.4 Social media: locating job opportunities

Social media such as LinkedIn, Facebook, Google Plus and Twitter are becoming key online ways for employers to fill new positions. Likewise, they are becoming the key ways for those seeking jobs and locating prospective opportunities. LinkedIn is the principal professional career-related social media site for careers in a number of countries.

Use LinkedIn (or other similar platforms that are key websites) to locate job opportunities in your preferred career or profession. Check out opportunities for related jobs to your preferred graduate position. Look for opportunities in allied areas if the job market is poor in your chosen career area or locality.

Ensure you are visible so that prospective employers can see you on these social media career sites in terms of a graduate seeking employment in your career area.

Social Media: Locating Job Opportunities

Career Profiles (a US career and job search company) advises:

> Companies actually hire through LinkedIn, and with good reason. LinkedIn profiles make the hiring process much easier for companies, who can see immediately who the most qualified, most recommended candidates are before even announcing the job opening. The trick, then, is to be visible and easily findable to those companies searching for new recruits.

Companies search the LinkedIn database for specific skills, experience and keywords:

> If you had entered that information onto your profile, you would show up in their search, and you may very well be contacted for an interview. This is why it's important to be thorough as you fill in your information; you never know what keyword could be the ticket to your next interview.

Career Profiles advises on the importance of social networking when looking for a job. The US Bureau of Labor Statistics reports that 70% of all jobs are found through networking: "There are a number of online resources designed just for this purpose, and learning to use them effectively will put you at a real advantage in today's competitive job market."

See Career Profiles, www.careerprofiles.info, in the References at the end of this chapter.

Create a Social Media Profile for Job Searching

5.2.4.1   Create a social media profile for job searching

Creating a profile or bio (biography) on social media platforms such as LinkedIn, Facebook, Google Plus and Twitter, is similar to posting your

48

resume. It is your online professional image and the way you present yourself to the professional world. It needs to be sufficiently detailed and present a quality image. In effect, it is your online resume. It should reflect your qualifications, experience and personal skills.

Once you have assessed the options for different social media (such as LinkedIn, Facebook, Google Plus and Twitter) for job searching, you can move to the next stage of signing up and establishing a profile (bio).

Having a presence on social media that focuses on your career and job search is a valuable investment. Social media is used by employers to advertise and fill new positions. It is also a key way for you to expand your job search/job hunting reach.

5.2.4.2 How to be visible on LinkedIn

How to Be Visible on LinkedIn

Companies search the LinkedIn database for specific skills, experience, and keywords:

> If you had entered that information onto your profile, you would show up in their search, and you may very well be contacted for an interview. This is why it's important to be thorough as you fill in your information.

> Incorporating keywords into your resume and profile is crucial for being found.

To find out which keywords will be particularly useful for you, read some actual job advertisements and postings. Identify the key job criteria and the keywords. Ensure they appear in your profile (online resume) as part of your qualifications, experience or personal characteristics.

See Career Profiles, www.careerprofiles.info, in the References at the end of this chapter.

5.2.4.3 Social media for job hunting

Use social media as a key aspect of your job hunting. Some, such as LinkedIn, focus on professions and careers. Others, such as Facebook,

Google Plus or Twitter, are widening beyond social interactions and increasing their presence in the job search area.

Have a profile on the social media site(s) you have chosen to focus on. Companies search the LinkedIn database for specific skills, experience and keywords. You want them to know about you and your capabilities.

Use social media for your searches for job openings and opportunities; for example, LinkedIn's search engine can be an advantage. You can search by keywords, professional titles or industries. It will locate professionals in your prospective career area. Searching for jobs by company is also possible. Your opportunities will increase.

For job applications directly through LinkedIn, your LinkedIn profile (online resume) is sent to the hiring manager; therefore, ensure your profile (online resume) is up to date and professional.

With Facebook, you will need to decide whether to expand it from a social presence into a professional presence. Facebook has options of adjusting who can see what on your profile.

Google Plus (with "Circles" and "Streams") can help in job searching other networking sites. It permits you to keep your social and professional contacts (and updates) separate. It makes it easier to establish a professional network and make useful connections.

The following chapters will outline:

- Chapter 6: Social media – job search options.

- Chapter 7: Social media – establishing your online profile.

- Chapter 8: Social media for job hunting.

They provide an overview of LinkedIn, Facebook, Google Plus and Twitter for job searching.

Social Media → For Career & Professional Use → Identifies you as a job seeker → Helps locates job opportunities

5.2.5 Advertisements: press

Printed job advertisements are an older methodology that is has become largely outdated. It has been overtaken by online options; some are provided by newspapers offering online job listings.

It is cumbersome to locate newspapers, choose which papers to scan, and which region, state or national level to pursue jobs. Online job listings via newspapers are far more convenient.

Professional journals can also carry advertisements for positions. Mostly these will be for very specialised positions or senior roles.

5.2.6 *Online Internet opportunities*

Job vacancies are advertised online. Commercial organisations offer this service to both employers and employees.

Human resource organisations consolidate job openings and opportunities via their websites. They offer search engine tools to narrow jobs to professions, qualifications and locality.

See Search for online job search sites in your region; for example, www.seek.com; www.careerone.com.au; and www.indeed.com in the References at the end of this chapter.

Each country or region will have different organisations in this job search area. Tap into this market area to locate job opportunities.

Your choice of your region for job searching is important. How widely are you searching? Locally, regionally, state-wide or nationally? The wider the area of your search, the more opportunities become available; this will increase your chances of successfully finding a job, as long as you are willing to take up an employment opportunity further from home. This is a powerful Internet area for job searching. LinkedIn already has a dominant presence in the social media area (for careers and profession); others such as Facebook Careers, Google Plus or Twitter are expanding in this area. Locate the dominant social media website for your region.

5.2.7 Job search agencies (servicing employers)

These organisations provide a service to employers. Their role is to provide professional human resource skills and services. Employers may prefer to use these agencies to reduce a manager's workload that is required to fill a vacancy. Your job search opportunities are increased by linking into and monitoring these organisations in your region, state or nationally for job openings.

5.2.8 Job search agencies (servicing potential employees): commercial

This service is directed towards those who are seeking a job. The agency's role is to help you find the right job for you and to help you to win. In some cases, these commercial organisations may be operating on behalf government employment agencies. Such employment agencies can also be useful for short-term employment while you are waiting to find a permanent job.

5.2.9 Job search agencies (servicing potential employees): government

This is a service provided by governments. It may occur at the regional, state and national levels. Sometimes these may be operated by commercial organisations contracted by government departments. These agencies usually offer a wide range of services: job search advice, job application assistance and other support services for those seeking employment. Therefore, it may include assistance with resumes, application letters and overall guidance. Their role is to help you find a job. The overall aim of such organisations includes: reducing unemployment, helping jobseekers and assisting business development with employment.

5.2.9.1 Group discussion/tutorial

Discuss the following:

- Different job market services are available. Which offer the best potential to increase your job opportunities?

- Is there one that stands out to for you to use?
- Should you seek professional advice on job markets?
- What is the potential of social media for job searching?

5.2.10   Non-advertised jobs

With the increased trend to social media for careers and job opportunities, it is possible for employers to now fill vacancies without advertising or using job listings. Those seeking positions will have their profiles (bio) up on a social media platform (e.g. LinkedIn) and are visible to employers seeking to recruit a suitable person. Companies search the LinkedIn database for specific skills, experience and keywords. Ensure your profile is complete.

Of course, one can also make an unsolicited job application. For example, if there is an employer in your area where you would like to work, and for which you consider that you have the relevant qualifications, you can simply make a cold call to the company and approach the personnel manager (or human resources) to present your resume and ask if there are any job opportunities. Often they will appreciate your initiative, if they happen to have a vacancy at that point in time. Of course, you should have done your homework about that company beforehand, so you know what they do and activities in your career area.

5.2.11   Networking: job opportunities

Professional networking includes linking into activities and discussions related to your profession.

The next three chapters are entirely devoted to showing you how to use social media to find and obtain a job. As you will read there, social media sites such as LinkedIn, Facebook, Google Plus and Twitter are a very powerful tool for professional networking, as they all have discussion groups and you can follow the posts of influential business leaders. Hence, it is not surprising that many jobs are filled by networking, where roles are filled without advertising. It increases as employers use online websites that list profiles (bios) of those seeking positions.

This is a possible area to widen your search for a job opportunity. Networking is basically building your range of contacts so your availability is known and you learn of upcoming openings for graduates.

5.2.12 Job fairs

Job fairs offer you a helping hand, supporting you in beginning your career. Exhibitors at such job fairs typically include international companies looking to recruit young talent and recruitment agencies. At job fairs, you can talk one-to-one with recruiters and get professional advice. It will give you valuable insights into career opportunities. Just type in "job fairs" and "(your region)" into your Internet browser and you will find many. In the USA and Europe, most universities will offer such a job fair on a regular basis to help their graduates find a job. Also, many local and regional government agencies also organise such events to attract young graduates to come and work in their province or city.

See the job fair websites listed in the References at the end of this chapter.

5.2.13 Personal Plan: locating job opportunities

To download the eResource digital Appendices: Personal Plan, follow the instructions in the References at the end of the chapter.

In your Personal Plan you will identify:

- Different job market sectors.
- Which ones offer the best potential for job opportunities.
- Which ones stand out to you for added attention and to use.
- Seeking professional advice on this.
- Using social media.

Complete Appendix: Personal Plan 5: locating Jobs.

5.2.14 Networking: approaching organisations

This approach has been overtaken by Internet and social media platforms.

The purpose of networking in the past was to link you into potential organisations and explore employment opportunities.

The approach was not about writing to an organisation and asking for a job; it involved a more subtle approach. This involved asking for career advice or potential contacts – for them to recommend organisations in your chosen profession. In addition, you may have included a short version of your resume for reference.

In many organisations it was very hard to get past the receptionist or personal secretary to talk with the manager. Nowadays use the organisation's website to talk with the manager, receptionist or personal secretary. Ask them who would be the best person to contact to obtain advice regarding key contacts in the industry for new graduates. Many people are willing to help a young graduate get started.

The aim is to get them to provide a suggested contact: the person's name, the organisation's address or the email. At this stage your letter moves from a more general Dear Sir/Dear Madam to Dear (recommended manager's name). This means it is directed to the right person. It also has a personal touch – the person's name.

The approach is to ask the manager for their professional advice by asking them who would be valuable contacts for you to follow up within the industry or profession. You are seeking to contact key people who can provide helpful advice to a new graduate in your career area or profession. You introduce yourself by saying you recognise that their experience and professional standing will give them a wider insight into this area. You would appreciate any advice or contacts (other organisations) that they can offer. Adding: I have attached a short resume to give you an outline my capabilities to assist you. I would appreciate your assistance and professional advice.

Identify contacts	Build networks	Seek advice & guidance	Locate new job opportunities

It was a way to provide organisations with your interest via your short resume and your contact letter. The aim was to have your job interest on their record. In addition, the intent was to obtain a referral to another organisation or one of their key contacts.

Primarily, it helped target the person to contact in the other organisation. It gave a personalised approach by using their name and the name of the person who recommended you contact them. It had more impact than a generalised letter to the overall organisation.

This changed the approach letter (which was seeking advice) from a generalised, impersonal letter to a specific letter to a specific individual.

Your letter included:

Dear [Name]

Your name has been suggested as a key contact in (industry or career area). (Add in recommending person's name) has suggested that I contact you. They have suggested that you would be a valuable source for professional advice. I would appreciate your assistance and advice on any organisations I should contact. I am a young graduate seeking employment and career in the area of (industry or career area).

Would you be able to suggest any key professional persons or any other organisations that I could contact for guidance on career opportunities? I would appreciate professional advice and help.

Yours sincerely,
PS. I have attached a short version of my resume.

This approach does not put them on the spot in terms of directly asking for a job. It taps into their recognition in being recommended by someone else in their profession. Most people value recognition and being asked for their professional advice.

The key points from the networking and approaching organisations letter include:

- Make it personal (name of key contact if discovered).
- Ask for their professional advice.
- Advise you are searching for a job opportunity to start your career.
- Ask for any personal or professional contacts that they may suggest.
- Ask for any organisations they feel worth contacting.
- Include a copy of a short resume for reference.
- Thank them.

This approach opened networking and job opportunities in the past. With the Internet and social media sites such as LinkedIn that focus on professions and careers, it has been superseded.

Your approach nowadays will largely be via the Internet, social media platforms (career related) and discussion groups where you can seek advice.

5.3 Summary

From this chapter you will now have the ability to identify a range of areas to seek job opportunities. Your scope for potential jobs has widened. In addition, you have learnt about organisations that can potentially help you in your search.

The importance of seeking advice and guidance – to ask and to listen – is significant. Put aside any reluctance. There are specialised job search agencies that exist to help fill job openings and can help you locate the right job. The importance of seeking advice and guidance from professionals in the job search area is significant.

Your Personal Plan: locating job opportunities has focused your priorities: which types of job search agencies are best for you? Which will you use? What actions do you intend to take?

It has provided an introduction to social media for job searching. It has focused on your broader plans for using social media: what are the barriers and opportunities? What are your initial plans to use social media for job hunting?

The more relevant the job opportunities that you identify, the greater are your chances. As one optimistic job seeker said, when faced with the tough statistical average for his area of 40 applications before getting a job: "That's application 30; I only need 10 more and I'll get that job!" Keep going!

You will have discovered a wider range of areas to seek job opportunities. The book aims to help you understand the main job location sectors.

In the following chapters we will look at:

- Chapter 6: social media – job search options.
  - Social media such as LinkedIn, Facebook, Google Plus and Twitter.
- Chapter 7: social media – establishing your online profile.
- Chapter 8: social media for job hunting.

5.4 References and further reading

Career Profiles. Job searching social networking sites. www.careerprofiles. info

Gregory, M. (2008) *The Career Chronicles: An Insider's Guide to What Jobs Are Really Like – the Good, the Bad and the Ugly from Over 750 Professionals* (New World Library, California).

Search for online job search sites in your region. (e.g. www.seek.com; www.careerone.com.au; www.indeed.com).

Job fair websites: https://careers.umd.edu

www.expatfair.nl

www.careerfairs.psu.edu

www.mainecareercenter.gov/employment/jobfairs.shtml

Or via the short cut: https://tinyurl.com/m6q675n

The references above are available for direct links on the eResource website.

5.4.1 Reference: eResources link for this book

For added resources and digital files related to this chapter:

Search: Routledge Text Books or go to: www.routledge.com/

Search window: type "Your Career" and it will take you to the eResources for this book.

Or via the short cut: https://tinyurl.com/kyxnfaq

Then go to the Appendices <TAB> and the Personal Plan <TAB> (Appendices: Personal Plan) and follow the download instructions. Then save it to a working folder on your PC.

6 Social media
Job search options

6.1 Introduction

We will now explore the online social media platforms for job searching. These include LinkedIn, Facebook, Google Plus and Twitter. In different countries, others may have key roles.

Social Media for Job Search

In this chapter you will see how employers use social media platforms to locate potential employees or job seekers. Social media options for your job searching are compared and reviewed. The aim is to give you an understanding of some main social media platforms for job hunting. Other platforms may be significant in different countries or regions. Select the ones that are dominant in your area.

6.2 Social media: job search options

6.2.1 Employers' use of social media for employment

Social media such as LinkedIn, Facebook, Google Plus and Twitter are becoming key online ways for employers to advertise and fill new positions. Likewise, they are becoming the key ways for those seeking jobs.

Career Profiles (a US career and job search company) advises:

- Companies actually hire through LinkedIn.
- Reason: LinkedIn profiles make the hiring process much easier for companies.
- Companies can easily find who the most qualified and most recommended candidates are before announcing a job opening.
- Career Profiles recommend job searchers to be visible and easily findable to companies recruiting.

Employers' Use of Social Media for Employment

Companies search the LinkedIn database for specific skills, experience and keywords. The best advice is to ensure you have entered that information onto your profile. That way, you show up in their search; this increases your chance of getting an interview. Keywords in your profile are important.

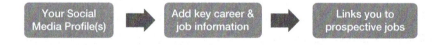

See Career Profiles, *Job Searching Social Networking Sites*, in the References at the end of this chapter.

Susan P. Joyce advises that social media can provide employers and recruiters with an indication of the following:

- Communication skills (including spelling and grammar).
- Work history and education.
- Knowledge of the industry.
- Alcohol and illegal substance use.
- Use of profanities.
- Non-work activities.

See Joyce: *Guide to Social Media and Job Search*, in the References at the end of this chapter.

6.2.2 Social media for job search: your options

Your Use of Social Media for Job Search

Job hunting today has moved from newspapers and online jobs board search to social media.

Job seekers can now connect with and attract potential employers. Your first contact with a potential employer is most likely through the Internet.

Susan P. Joyce provides advice:

- "Social media and social networking are the rage right now in business and in private life."
- "Job search is a large portion of what is happening."
- Social media provides a quick and inexpensive background check (done before inviting a person for a job interview).
- Employers use social media to verify the facts on resumes and check communications skills.

See Joyce: *Guide to Social Media and Job Search*, in the References at the end of this chapter.

LinkedIn is the principal social network for job searching. Career advisors recommend that if you only use one social network for your job search, LinkedIn is the one to use.

Recognise the benefits of Social Media for Job Search

Explore its capabilities

Social networks are increasingly being used by recruiters and job boards are now used less. LinkedIn continues to dominate social networks used for recruiting. Facebook is popular generally, but it is less popular for finding job seekers. It is often used to promote an employer as a positive place to work. A Jobvite.com survey of 800 US employers in 2013 asked whether they were using or planning to use social media for their recruiting; 94% of employers said they were (increasing from 78% of employers in 2008).

Social media helps recruiters obtain a better picture of applicants even before talking to them. It provides information about an applicant's personality and how they might fit into their corporate culture.

See Jobvite.com, *Social Recruiting 2013 Survey Results* and Joyce, *Guide to Social Media and Job Search*, in the References at the end of this chapter.

The US Bureau of Labor Statistics reports that 70% of all jobs are found through networking. Career Profiles advises on the importance of social networking when looking for a job. It advises job searchers to utilise available online resources to gain an advantage in a competitive job market.

See Career Profiles, *Job Searching Social Networking Sites*, in the References at the end of this chapter.

Social media can provide information and connections that are vital to your job search. You can research companies and industries. The University of Buffalo, New York, School of Management outlines these:

- Connections: identify alumni at your target companies.

- Company information: learn about the company's culture, hiring process, corporate values and recruiting.

- Industry information: see competitors and understand how skills transfer within the industry.

- Job information: see career paths for various functions and review job postings.

See University of Buffalo, New York, School of Management, *How to Effectively Use Social Media in Your Job Search*, in the References at the end of this chapter.

6.2.3   LinkedIn

LinkedIn for Job Hunting

Susan P. Joyce advises on the major social media associated with job searching:

- LinkedIn is the professional's social network.
- LinkedIn is the network preferred by most employers.
- It provides professional interconnection, group forums and interaction.
- LinkedIn has over 500 million members (2017).
- Check out the Guide to LinkedIn for Job Search for help maximising LinkedIn.
- Join the Job Hunt Help LinkedIn Group for help with your job search.

See Joyce, *Guide to Social Media and Job Search*, in the References at the end of this chapter.
    Career Profiles advises:

- LinkedIn is useful for companies in the process of hiring new employees. It allows them to browse an online profile and rapidly find the most appealing people for the position.
- The network you build on LinkedIn can become an important source of information and opportunities.
- Sign up to LinkedIn as it is easy and fast.
- Create a profile after you are registered.
- Ensure your profile is well crafted and thoughtfully presented.

See Career Profiles, *Job Searching Social Networking Sites*, in the References at the end of this chapter. The University of Buffalo, School of Management advises:

- LinkedIn is a business-oriented social network that connects millions of professionals.

- "It provides the largest opportunity to market yourself and expand your personal network."
- "Your LinkedIn profile provides a visible, online resume that your contacts, including potential employers, can view."

See University of Buffalo, New York, School of Management, *How to Effectively Use Social Media in Your Job Search*, in the References at the end of this chapter.

6.2.4   Facebook

Facebook is the largest social networking website. It permits users to join networks in their city, region or workplace. It has over 2 billion members worldwide (2017). It can be a tool for job searches.

Facebook for Job Hunting

Some useful Facebook advice includes:

- Many large organisations utilise Facebook as part of their graduate recruitment strategy.
- You also can use Facebook (or LinkedIn) to research hiring managers.
- Use your Facebook network to reflect your job search goals.

See Morgan, *9 Tips to Leverage Facebook for a Successful Job Search*, in the References at the end of this chapter.

6.2.4.1   Facebook for job seekers

Explore options to use Facebook to link to other professionals in your career area and to grow your network.

- Check your privacy settings; select the best option to reflect what you want people to see.

- Complete your profile: complete your "About" section to reflect your profession and career directions.

- Check Facebook status update settings: what people can or cannot see (public, friends, other).

- Facebook lists: you can choose who sees an update.

- Follow people of interest in your profession or career area.

- Discover job leads: search for "jobs" and your "city" for leads.

- Interact with your network: post updates related to your job search.

See Job Hunt, *Facebook Job Search*, in the References at the end of this chapter.

6.2.4.2   Facebook for networking?

Facebook for Networking

The fact that there are several hundred million users of Facebook indicates its potential value. The key question is: can you really get a job with Facebook?

The Undercover Recruiter suggests some possible benefits of Facebook:

- Networking: recruiters and prospective new employers will be on Facebook.

- Network yourself to whoever is hiring at the moment.

- Use Facebook for a job hunt and update your status with your current situation and what you are looking for.

- Check out Facebook marketplace: online marketplaces can help in your job hunt. Look through the marketplace for job listings you can apply for.

- Join groups and be active, similar to LinkedIn groups. The aim is to network and locate opportunities.

See The Undercover Recruiter, *How to Use Facebook to Get Hired [5 Ways]*, in the References at the end of this chapter.

While Facebook is not in the same category as LinkedIn regarding careers, it may be another job search strategy to consider. It is important to remember that potential employers will no doubt also check you out on Facebook, once you have applied for a job in their organisation. They can see what type of person you are, by the nature and type of photos, messages and other activities you do on Facebook.

Job hunting is undergoing another big change in the world of social media. Job seekers are utilising the big social networks in ingenious ways to find jobs. The Undercover Recruiter indicates that this is successful as "the more you use a social network, the more likely you are to find a job through the service: 1 in 4 'super social (job) seekers' successfully network through Facebook, Twitter, or LinkedIn".

See The Undercover Recruiter, *How to Use Facebook to Get Hired [5 Ways]*, in the References at the end of this chapter.

6.2.4.3   Facebook for job searching?

Link Humans (a US social media and marketing company) conducted a survey to understand whether people use Facebook when looking for a job and how they would use it.

> In a nutshell – you'll find out that people don't really use Facebook to find a job but they would definitely do it to get more information about a company. All these results allow us to deduct Facebook has a personal use and private use. Job seekers tend to use other social platforms like LinkedIn more, the number one professional social network.

See Link Humans, *How People Use Facebook in Their Job Searches*, in the References at the end of this chapter.

6.2.4.4   Facebook careers advice to job seekers

Explore potential employer's Facebook pages for opportunities. These may be listed as:

- Work opportunities.
- University graduate positions.
- Internships.
- Contractor opportunities.
- Careers.
- Identify potential jobs. Follow links to "Apply now".

See Facebook, *Facebook Careers*, in the references at the end of this chapter.

6.2.5   *Google Plus*

Google Plus (also known as Google +) has around 111 million members (early 2017). It allows "Circles" (private, user-defined groups of contacts), "Hangouts" (free user-created video chats) and "Communities" (social groups).

See Joyce, *Guide to Using Google for your Job Search*, in the References at the end of this chapter.

Google+ for Job Hunting

Google Plus is a social networking site. It is similar to Facebook, but with differences that can be useful for job searching. It allows:

- Personal profile (online resume).
- Networking professionally and searching for jobs.

- Google Plus "Circles" allows you to keep your social networking and your professional networking distinct from each other; this protects your privacy and social life.

- Google Plus "Streams" allows you to control who sees a post.

See Career Profiles, *Job Searching Social Networking Sites*, in the References at the end of this chapter.

Explore Google Plus ⟩ Explore its capabilities for job search

6.2.6 *Twitter*

Can Twitter be useful in job searching? It is a social networking service that allows users to exchange messages called tweets. These are short messages of 140 characters, although this has recently been doubled to 280 characters.

Tweets are delivered to the users (subscribers). It can play a role in job hunting. Twitter can be used by individuals and companies for short communications including job searching and professional networking.

It is important to remember that potential employers may look at your Twitter history to see what type of person you are, so delete any messages that you do not want them to see before applying for a job.

See Job Hunt, *Guide to Twitter for Job Search*, in the References at the end of this chapter.

Twitter for Job Hunting

Career Profiles advises:

> These days, most companies have their own Twitter accounts, which they use to update their followers about special offers, sales, or job openings. A good way to find job opportunities, then, is to check out the Twitter accounts of the companies you're interested in working for, follow their tweets, and stay updated as they post job openings.

> TwitJobSearch.com is a valuable resource for the job seeker. It's a Twitter-specific search engine, which allows you to search the site for job opportunities by keyword (such as 'paralegal London' or 'tech journalist USA').

See Career Profiles, *Job Searching Social Networking Sites*, in the References at the end of this chapter.

Some useful advice includes:

- Use a separate professional Twitter account.
- Make the 140 characters of your bio count; be specific about what you have to offer and what you are looking for.
- Follow industry experts and organisations you are interested in; participate in discussions.
- Link to your online profiles (such as LinkedIn).

6.3 Summary

This chapter has introduced social media options for job searching. You have explored employers' use of social media for employment. You have been given an overview of some major social media platforms. These have included LinkedIn, Facebook, Google Plus and Twitter. In the next chapter, you will be introduced to using social media to establish your online profile (biography or bio).

6.4 References and further reading

Career Profiles, *Job Searching Social Networking Sites*. www.careerprofiles. info/job-searching-social-networking-sites.html or via the short cut: https://tinyurl.com/lbegdnt

Facebook, *Facebook Careers*. www.facebook.com/careers/

Morgan, H. *9 Tips to Leverage Facebook for a Successful Job Search*. Job Hunt. www.job-hunt.org/social-networking/facebook-job-search.shtml or via the short cut: https://tinyurl.com/36qrqax

Jobvite.com, *Social Recruiting Survey Results 2013*. http://web.jobvite.com/ rs/jobvite/images/Jobvite_2013_SocialRecruitingSurveyResults.pdf or via the short cut: https://tinyurl.com/m2sjjo6

Joyce, S.P., *Guide to Facebook for Job Search*. Job Hunt. www.job-hunt.org/facebook-job-search/facebook-job-search.shtml

Joyce, S.P., *Guide to Social Media and Job Search*. Job Hunt, www.job-hunt.org/social-networking/social-media.shtml

Joyce, S.P., *Guide to Twitter for Job Search*. Job Hunt, www.job-hunt.org/social-networking/twitter-job-search.shtml or via the short cut: https://tinyurl.com/k4qn5c5

Joyce, S.P., *Guide to Using Google for Your Job Search*. Job Hunt. www.job-hunt.org/guides/google/using-google.shtml

Joyce, S.P., *10 Twitter SEO Tips to Attract Recruiters*. Job Hunt, www.job-hunt.org/social-networking/twitter-job-search-SEO.shtml or via the short cut: https://tinyurl.com/laf4mbc

Link Humans, *How People Use Facebook in Their Job Searches*. www.linkhumans.com/blog/using-facebook-job-search or via the short cut: https://tinyurl.com/k5e8zak

Rose, A. (2016) *LinkedIn In 30 Minutes: How to Create a Rock-Solid LinkedIn Profile and Build Connections that Matter*. (i30 Media, Boston, MA, USA, 2nd edn).

The Undercover Recruiter, *How to Use Facebook to Get Hired [5 Ways]*. www.theundercoverrecruiter.com/5-ways-use-facebook-your-job-search/ or via the short cut: https://tinyurl.com/kovrekn

University of Buffalo, New York, School of Management, *How to Effectively Use Social Media in Your Job Search*. https://mgt.buffalo.edu/career-resource-center/students/networking/social-media/using.html or via the short cut: https://tinyurl.com/kryclth

These references are available for direct links on the eResource website.

6.4.1 Reference: eResources link for this book

For added resources and digital files related to this chapter:

Search: Routledge Text Books or go to: www.routledge.com/

Search window: type "Your Career" and it will then take you to the eResources for this book.

Or via the short cut: https://tinyurl.com/kyxnfaq

Then go to the Web References <TAB> then the References <TAB>.

Social media
Establishing your online profile

7.1 Introduction

This chapter provides an outline of the options available to set up your online social media profile. These cover the main platforms: LinkedIn, Facebook, Google Plus and Twitter. You can also choose other social media platforms that may be significant in your country or region.

7.2 Social media: establishing your online profile

Once you have assessed the options for different social media platforms for job searching, you can move to the next stage of signing up and establishing a bio (biographical) profile.

Social Media: Your Online Profile

Having a presence on social media that focuses on your career and job search is a valuable investment. It is used by employers to advertise and fill new positions. It is also a key way for you to expand your job hunting reach.

When looking at your social media online profile, check out the following things first, as these are what potential employers will do or see before they invite you to a job interview:

- Check your name on Google. What do you find? Is it the "real you" or are you not happy with how you are depicted? If not, then change it.
- Remove any inappropriate photos or messages on your various social media accounts.

- Check your postings or blog accounts. If you have any unfavourable items, delete them before you apply for a job.

- Check your privacy settings. Ensure your intimate personal conversations are not read by everyone.

- Keep your online profiles up to date and make them as professional as you can.

- Join in discussion groups on social media networks, especially ones related to your future employment fields.

- Check your spelling and grammar before posting an item or message on your social media networks. It reflects on you and the way you express yourself.

7.3 LinkedIn profile

Career Profiles advises:

> It is your online professional image and the way you present yourself to the professional world. It needs to be sufficiently detailed and present a quality image. In effect it's your online resume. It should reflect your qualifications, experience and personal achievements.

Think about the name of your account on social media sites. Perhaps reconsider your "student account name" now that you want to enter the job market. Names you used as a student may no longer be appropriate, so change it to something more suitable.

7.3.1 Your profile photo

Use a professional photo, not any holiday photo.

LinkedIn (Bio) Profile

7.3.2 LinkedIn profile: connect with the professional world

Make sure your profile is public so others can see it. Career Profiles advises:

- Customise your url (the actual web address which appears in your browser bar). This can make your profile much easier to share with other professionals. The alternative can be long and incomprehensible.

- Check and see if you can change it to your name and career. LinkedIn advises which options are available and which are not.

- A summary can be added to your profile. This should include several paragraphs about your professional strengths, experience, skills and training. Ideally it should be easy for employers to scan or read quickly.

- Select your industry: at the beginning of your profile, next to your photo and name, you can create a headline and choose an industry. This is important, as it is how companies search for prospective employees. The aim is to ensure you can be found easily.

- "Experience" section: add appropriate information that describes your skills and qualifications. This is like an online resume. Include work experience as well as any volunteer work experience.

- "Additional information" in your profile can show other social media links or resources you think prospective employers would like to see. Present a quality picture of yourself to the world.

See Career Profiles, *Job Searching Social Networking Sites*, in the References at the end of this chapter.

7.3.3 Personal Plan: social media profile

To download the eResource digital Appendices: Personal Plan, follow the instructions in the References at the end of the chapter.

See Appendix Personal Plan 6: social media profile

- Profile url.
- Photo.
- Summary of profile.
- Industry.
- Experience.

Now commence your Personal Plan for your online social media profile. You can progressively work through this.

Create a professional LinkedIn Profile → Connect to your professional world → Connect to your career area

7.3.4 *Referees and recommendations*

LinkedIn has the advantage and ability to request recommendations from contacts, affiliates, current and former supervisors, etc. These recommendations serve as references for potential employers. A profile with several positive recommendations from other professionals carries added weight for those interviewing and selecting applicants.

Writing a recommendation takes time. A positive suggestion is for you to write a draft version for them first. Be honest and realistic. Request recommendations from previous supervisors and co-workers. It will add to your profile.

7.3.5 *How to be visible on LinkedIn*

Career Profiles advises:

- LinkedIn profiles make hiring much easier for companies; they can see qualified and recommended candidates before even announcing the job opening.
- Companies actually hire through LinkedIn.
- Be visible and easily findable for companies searching for new recruits.

Companies search the LinkedIn database for specific skills, experience and keywords. Ensure you enter keywords into your profile that relate to your career and the job you are seeking. These are crucial links to help employers find you.

See Career Profiles, *Job Searching Social Networking Sites*, in the references at the end of this chapter.

Be Visible on LinkedIn

To find out which keywords will be particularly useful for you, read some actual job advertisements and postings. Identify the key job criteria – the keywords. Ensure they appear in your profile (online resume) as part of your qualifications, experience or personal characteristics. University of Buffalo, New York, School of Management recommends a complete and strong profile. They advise:

- A complete profile makes you 40 times more likely to receive job opportunities.

- A potential employer is looking for useful information about potential employees.

- Including major accomplishments, experiences, education, skills, honours and any other professional achievements you would include on a resume or in an interview.

- Use a professional picture of yourself for your profile image.

- Make sure whatever you do on LinkedIn is professional and appropriate; do not forget that potential employers will be seeing it.

See University of Buffalo, New York, School of Management, *How to Effectively Use Social Media in your Job Search*, in the References at the end of this chapter.

For your LinkedIn profile, use the most professional photo you have of yourself; avoid selfies.

See Morgan, *9 Tips to Leverage Facebook for a Successful Job Search*, in the References at the end of this chapter.

Specialists in Recruitment → Recommend LinkedIn → Use it for Job Hunting

7.4 Facebook profile

Facebook Profile

Facebook Careers provides a range of useful advice to job seekers. Explore a potential employer's Facebook pages for opportunities. Follow links to "Apply now". Details may include:

- Personal details.
- Attach resume.
- Attach cover letter.
- "Tell us in 300 characters or less something that can't be found on your resume that makes you an ideal candidate for this job."
- Facebook url.
- Further personal details.
- "What makes you unique? In 150 characters or fewer, tell us what makes you unique. Try to be creative and say something that will catch our eye!"
- Submit application.

See Facebook, *Facebook Careers*, in the References at the end of this chapter.

Other aspects on top of your resume and cover letter may request short statements about you. Why are you the ideal candidate? What makes you unique? These can specify brevity. If not, keep them short and direct. If the request is for a 300 characters limit, this is:

- six short sentences as bullet points; or
- four lines.

If the request is for a 150 characters limit, this is:

- three short sentences as bullet points; or
- two lines.

7.4.1 Ideal candidate?

If you are requested to provide a short selling statement on why you are the ideal candidate, this is about marketing yourself. It is about attracting the reviewer's attention to your application. It is about getting to the point.

A later resource you will develop and can use will be your Foundation Resume. The achievement statements you will develop in later chapters are likely to be too much detail. The aim will be to select key selling points that make you the ideal candidate.

In effect it will be a summary of your resume or job application in two to four lines or three to six bullet point sentences. Base it on the main job requirement. Write it. Review it. Get another person's opinion. Imagine you are the application reviewer: does it sell you as the ideal person?

7.4.2 What makes you unique?

If you are requested to provide a short selling statement on what makes you different, this is also about marketing yourself. It is about attracting the reviewer's attention to your application.

You have just two to four lines or three to six bullet point sentences to make the point.

Base it on your personal abilities – things that make you stand out from others. Write it. Review it. Get another person's opinion. Imagine you are the application reviewer: does it show you as the unique person you really are?

See Facebook, *Facebook Careers*, in the References at the end of this chapter.

7.4.3 Check your Facebook profile and image

Employers do social network checks, so review your site and your profile. Change privacy settings to remove inappropriate material.

7.5 Google Plus profile

Google Plus is a social networking site. It is similar to Facebook, but with differences that can be useful for job searching. Advice from Career Profiles includes:

- Create a profile.
- To network professionally and search for jobs, let your profile reflect that.
- Use a professional-looking photo.
- Provide your educational background and professional work experience.
- Outline briefly your accomplishments, interests and volunteer experience; include other information you think an employer may want to see.
- Create the best impression via your profile for your new professional contacts.

See Career Profiles, *Job Searching Social Networking Sites*, in the References at the end of this chapter.

7.6 Twitter profile

You only have 140 characters (upgrading to 280) to tell them everything they need to know; therefore, it has to be convincing and every letter needs to count.

Recruiters and potential employers search Google for job candidates. Google links to Twitter. The aim is to make it easy for potential employers or job openings to link to you. By using search engine optimisation techniques it makes it easier for you to connect. This applies for Twitter, Google and other search engines.

Twitter Profile

Advice from Susan P. Joyce (Job Hunt) includes:

● Ensure you can be found on Twitter if someone does a search on you, the job title you want, your profession and your name. Use the right keywords.

● Ensure your Twitter account can be found if someone Googles your name.

7.6.1 Twitter username options

You can use your real name and your profession for your Twitter username. Your Twitter username establishes your Twitter url (e.g. twitter.com/John Smith) and is your public name in tweets (e.g. @John Smith). Twitter allows a maximum of 15 letters and numbers in this field. Spaces are not allowed but underscores can be used to separate words, letters or numbers. Your name is usually a straightforward option, especially if your name plus profession cannot readily be included in the 15 character limit.

Your name + professional designation:

● It could already be taken by someone else.

● Adding a professional designation strengthens your professional identity. (e.g. (name) eng)

● Your profession: if this is the option you choose, then use your actual name in the name field to help Twitter and Google connect the two.

Twitter Account Name

7.6.2 Twitter account name

The words you select and the order of the words in your Twitter profile page title are important for search engines and Twitter search. Put the most important keywords first; this may be your profession and location. You are selecting keywords you want to describe you. As an example: Peter S Smith Eng (PSSmithEng) reflects the Twitter name followed by the Twitter username.

7.6.3 Your location

Include where you are living or the location where you want to work. This is an important keyword for job seekers. It is used by recruiters when searching for candidates.

7.6.4 Your Twitter bio, photo and link

- Use relevant keyword-rich information in your bio.
- Add the url for your LinkedIn profile to your bio.
- Use your LinkedIn profile photo in your Twitter account – it shows that the two accounts are from the same person.

Use keywords an employer would use in a search for prospective employees. You have 160 characters for your bio. For example (keywords in bold):

Recent **college grad, accounting major**, seeking **entry level financial job. Work experience during degree**. Prefer (location).

See Joyce, *Twitter Job Search*, in the References at the end of this chapter.

7.7 Summary

This chapter has outlined how to set up your social media bio (biography) on different social media platforms. You can create your online bio now or you can wait and use Personal Plan materials you will complete in later chapters on achievement statements or later in your Foundation Resume.

This chapter has explored some of the main social media platforms including LinkedIn, Facebook, Google Plus and Twitter. You can also choose other social media platforms that may be significant in your country or region. Or Research Gate, if you are interested in looking for a job in academia or in a government research institute.

In the next chapter we will provide an outline of using social media for job hunting.

7.8 References and further reading

Cannon, J. (2004) *Find a Job: 7 Steps to Success.* (Cannon Career Development, Inc., Boston, MA).

Career Profiles, *Job Searching Social Networking Sites.* www.careerprofiles. info/job-searching-social-networking-sites.html or via the short cut: https://tinyurl.com/lbegdnt

Facebook, *Facebook Careers.* www.facebook.com/careers/

Jobvite, Social Recruiting 2013 Survey Results. http://web.jobvite.com/ rs/jobvite/images/Jobvite_2013_SocialRecruitingSurveyResults.pdf or via the short cut: https://tinyurl.com/m2sjjo6

Joyce, S.P., 10 Twitter SEO Tips to Attract Recruiters. Job Hunt, www. job-hunt.org/social-networking/twitter-job-search-SEO.shtml or via the short cut: https://tinyurl.com/laf4mbc

Joyce, S.P. *Guide to social Media and job Search.* Job Hunt, www. job-hunt.org/social-networking/social-media.shtml

Joyce, S.P., *Guide to Twitter for Job Search.* Job Hunt, www.job-hunt.org/social-networking/twitter-job-search.shtml or via the short cut: https://tinyurl.com/k4qn5c5

Joyce, S.P. *Guide to Using Google for your Job Search.* Job Hunt, www.job-hunt.org/guides/google/using-google.shtml

Link Humans, *How People Use Facebook in Their Job Searches.* www. linkhumans.com/blog/using-facebook-job-search or via the short cut: https://tinyurl.com/k5e8zak

Morgan, H. *9 Tips to Leverage Facebook for a Successful Job Search.* Job Hunt, www.job-hunt.org/social-networking/facebook-job-search.shtml

Rose, A. (2016) *LinkedIn in 30 Minutes: How to Create a Rock-Solid LinkedIn Profile and Build Connections that Matter* (i30 Media, Boston, MA, USA, 2nd edn).

The Undercover Recruiter, *How to Use Facebook to Get Hired [5 Ways]*. www.theundercoverrecruiter.com/5-ways-use-facebook-your-job-search/ or via the short cut: https://tinyurl.com/kovrekn

University of Buffalo, New York, School of Management, *How to Effectively use Social Media in your Job Search*. https://mgt.buffalo.edu/career-resource-center/students/networking/social-media/using.html or via the short cut: https://tinyurl.com/kryclth

These references are available for direct links on the eResource website.

7.8.1   Reference: eResources link for this book

For added resources and digital files related to this chapter:

Search: Routledge Text Books or go to: www.routledge.com/.

Search window: type "Your Career" which will take you to the eResources for this book.

Or via the short cut: https://tinyurl.com/kyxnfaq

Then go to the Web References <TAB> then the References <TAB>.

Social media for job hunting

8.1 Introduction

Opportunities to successfully gain a new position will be increased as you use social media for job hunting. In this chapter, techniques are reviewed for using LinkedIn, Facebook, Google Plus and Twitter. These offer the potential to identify new jobs and apply for them online.

You can choose other similar social media platforms if they are significant in your country.

8.2 Social media for job hunting

Use social media as a key aspect of your job hunting. It has become a key link for graduates seeking employment. The main site in many countries is LinkedIn, which has a profession and career focus. Other sites such as Facebook, Google Plus and Twitter are increasingly being used by employers and those seeking employment. Key words of advice from those with expertise in social media for job hunting are highlighted below.

Use Social Media for Job Hunting

8.3 LinkedIn

Career Profiles advises:

- Be visible and easily findable on LinkedIn.

- Companies hire through LinkedIn. The LinkedIn profiles make the hiring process much easier for companies. They can see immediately who the most qualified, most recommended candidates are (even before a job announcement).

- Companies search the LinkedIn database for specific skills, experience and keywords. Ensure your profile is complete. Including keywords in your resume and profile is crucial for being found.

To find out which keywords will be particularly useful for you, read some actual job advertisements and postings. Identify the key job criteria – the keywords. Ensure they appear in your profile (online resume) as part of your qualifications, experience or personal characteristics.

LinkedIn's search engine can be an advantage. You can search by keywords, professional titles or industries. It will locate professionals in your prospective career area. Possible opportunities increase as you connect with more people.

After you have completed your profile (online bio), LinkedIn provides a large number of job listings. You can then apply directly via the website.

Career Profiles advises on searching and applying for jobs using LinkedIn:

- Use the jobs link at top.
- Search field: key in job title, keyword or company name.
- Advanced search: this allows you to refine and filter your search based on an area, location, industry or position.
- Results appear. You can then sort by relevance or date.

Searching for jobs by company is possible (click on logos). Once you have identified a potential job listing, you can directly apply for the position via LinkedIn or via the company's website, or just save the job (and apply later).

LinkedIn allows you to view your saved jobs, share jobs via other networking sites such as Facebook or Twitter, or follow the company and receive regular updates.

For job applications directly through LinkedIn, your LinkedIn profile is sent to the hiring manager. Therefore, ensure your profile is up to date and professional.

Some company websites allow online applications. Follow the leads and submit a professional cover letter, resume and respond to key requested fields with short but good selling points.

To summarise, LinkedIn for job hunting (from Career Profiles):

- Is a powerful resource with a large number of tools for professional networking.
- Offers a large number of features, options and choices.
- Has options to join discussion groups, follow posts of influential business leaders.
- Enables sharing your own journey with your network.

Take your time and be patient as you learn the LinkedIn system. This is your professional image and should not be rushed.

See Career Profiles, *Job Searching Social Networking Sites*, in the References at the end of this chapter.

For LinkedIn job hunting:

- Search vacancies through LinkedIn jobs.
- Follow organisations you are interested in working for.
- Connect with industry job-seeking groups for search tips and opportunities.
- Collect skill endorsements and recommendations from colleagues, managers and other professionals who know your abilities.

The University of Buffalo, School of Management recommends growing your network:

- Start making connections as soon as your profile is complete.
- Import your address book to add people you know.
- Connect to friends, family, alumni, and past and present colleagues and supervisors.
- Try to add at least one new person to your network a week.
- When making a new connection, remind the individual of how you know each other.
- Quality is more important than quantity.
- Respond to requests promptly, within 24 hours if possible.
- Join LinkedIn groups that align with your professional interests, including alumni groups, trade associations and organisations of which you are a member.
- LinkedIn Jobs suggests open positions that align with your interests and allows you to search jobs based on different categories.
- Follow companies and industries in which you are interested.
- Research your recruiters or interviewers through their LinkedIn pages.

See University of Buffalo, New York, School of Management, *How to Effectively use Social Media in your Job Search*, in the References at the end of this chapter.

8.4 Facebook

Facebook is designed as a social networking site. Is it suitable or useful for professional networking and job searching? With Facebook's huge active user network worldwide, it is an avenue to connect with other people, ask for help, recommendations or advice.

Facebook is changing from just being a way to connect socially; it is also becoming viable to use it to search for job opportunities and careers. Explore ways you can use it for your job and career development.

Facebook for Job Hunting

Advice from Career Profiles includes:

- Decide if you want to keep Facebook as strictly social or widen its use into the professional area as well.

- If the latter, review what information is already on your profile, in particular, information you would not want employers to see.

- Facebook allows you to manage who sees your profile.

- Companies regularly check Facebook profiles of potential recruits prior to hiring.

Check that your profile on Facebook is the image you want to convey to potential employers. You can adjust the privacy settings of certain photos or comments to close friends only.

If professional networking and job searching is your primary purpose on Facebook, then simplify your profile to a professional, career focus and only post updates relevant to your career or your job search.

See Career Profiles, *Job Searching Social Networking Sites*, in the References at the end of this chapter.

Facebook is used more socially than professionally. It can be an added opportunity in job searching on top of LinkedIn. Make sure you are projecting a positive image via your online social media presence. More companies are using Facebook for recruiting and hiring. Follow companies you are interested in.

8.5 Google Plus

Google Plus is a social networking site. It is like Facebook, but with differences that can be useful for job searching.

After creating your Google Plus profile (online resume), Career Profiles advises the following:

- Google Plus "Circles" allows you to separate your contacts into different groups, such as "family", "friends" or "business".

- You can create and name your own "Circles" and place your contacts accordingly. People can even be placed in more than one "Circle" at a time. It allows you to separate your social network and your professional network. It also limits outside access.

- Google Plus "Streams" allows you to control who sees a post. You can limit viewing to certain "Circles" or certain individuals. You can switch between "Streams" by clicking the "Circle" you are focusing on.

Google Plus (with "Circles" and "Streams") can help in job searching other networking sites. It permits you to keep your social and professional contacts (and updates) separate. It makes it easier to establish a professional network and make useful connections.

> If you're seeking a job in a specific industry, search for contacts in that industry and add them to your "Circle". This will help you stay informed of emerging industry trends, new job postings, and other opportunities. Be sure to keep your "Circles" strategically separated, and post updates about the work you're hoping to find. As you expand your "Circles" and increase your contacts, more opportunities will become available to you. (from Career Profiles)

See Career Profiles, *Job Searching Social Networking Sites*, in the References at the end of this chapter.

8.6 Twitter

Twitter is traditionally used more socially than professionally. It can be an added opportunity in job searching on top of LinkedIn. Make sure you are projecting a positive image via your online social media presence. More companies are using Facebook and Twitter for recruiting and hiring. Follow companies you are interested in.

8.7 Other options

Blogs, websites and networking may provide helpful job search information. They may offer links to jobs, networking opportunities and relevant advice.

8.7.1 Websites: organising your job search

Website services are available which can assist you with an organisational system to keep track of job search information. They move you from a notebook approach towards a customer relationship software approach. The purpose is to remove the effort required to set up your own tracking and organisational system.

Check out the capabilities of the social media platform(s) you have chosen for managing your applications. You want to manage which openings you have applied for and track applications. Be willing to learn from unsuccessful ones and edit or update your profile if you think it is necessary. Make sure you are systematic and organised in your approach to job searching.

8.7.2 Networking is important

The role of social media in job searching is highlighted by Career Profiles, as follows:

- Many opportunities come from personal recommendations and connections.

- Be a visible member of the new online network of professionals.

- This network is global.

- Within this network, changes are constantly occurring and opportunities are constantly presenting themselves.

- Take advantage of these opportunities; tailor your online image and present yourself in a strategic way.

See Career Profiles, *Job Searching Social Networking Sites*, in the References at the end of this chapter.

What social media should you use? Several key ones have been outlined above; that is, LinkedIn, Facebook, Google Plus and Twitter. Each has strengths and weaknesses. It is smart to start with one and extend it to others to take advantage of possible job leads. LinkedIn has a focus on professions and careers and is the most significant platform in many countries. For your country, select the social media platform that is the most significant for careers.

Career Profiles also advises the following:

- Building a visible online presence on multiple online platforms. Most sites allow you to link your profiles together, so anyone who views your Twitter profile, for instance, can instantly navigate to your LinkedIn, Facebook and Google Plus profiles as well.

- Make it easy for a potential employer to link between your profiles, for example, from Facebook across to LinkedIn.

- Create an image that you would be proud to show an employer.

See Career Profiles, *Job Searching Social Networking Sites*, in the References at the end of this chapter.

The University of Buffalo, School of Management states the following:

> When used effectively and appropriately, social media can be one of your most valuable resources for career search and development. Use as many tools and resources as you can to become a pro at social networking.

See University of Buffalo, New York, School of Management, *How to Effectively use Social Media in your Job Search*, in the References at the end of this chapter.

8.8 Summary

Social media such as LinkedIn, Facebook, Google Plus or Twitter are becoming key online ways for employers to advertise and fill new positions. Likewise, they are becoming the key ways for those seeking jobs. They are powerful tools at your disposal.

Perhaps start with one platform such as LinkedIn and learn how it works: how you can use it to create a professional presence for yourself (profile) and to seek out job opportunities in your career area. You can expand to other platform options later if required.

Four main social media options for job hunting have been covered. These last three chapters on using social media to help find a job have offered you many practical tips.

In the next chapter we will focus on personal development. It will help you understand yourself. Decision-making tools will be given. These will help you work through complex options and hopefully make good job search choices.

8.9 References and further reading

Cannon, J. (2004) *Find a Job: 7 Steps to Success*. (Cannon Career Development, Inc., Boston, MA, USA).

Career Profiles, *Job Searching Social Networking Sites.* www.careerprofiles. info/job-searching-social-networking-sites.html or via the short cut: https://tinyurl.com/lbegdnt

Facebook, *Facebook Careers.* www.facebook.com/careers/

Jobvite, *Social Recruiting 2013 Survey Results.* http://web.jobvite.com/rs/ jobvite/images/Jobvite_2013_SocialRecruitingSurveyResults.pdf or via the short cut: https://tinyurl.com/m2sjjo6

Joyce, S.P., *10 Twitter SEO Tips to Attract Recruiters.* Job Hunt, www. job-hunt.org/social-networking/twitter-job-search-SEO.shtml or via the short cut: https://tinyurl.com/laf4mbc

Joyce, S.P., *Guide to Facebook for Job Search.* Job Hunt, www.job-hunt.org/facebook-job-search/facebook-job-search.shtml

Joyce, S.P., *Guide to social Media and job Search.* Job Hunt, www.job-hunt.org/social-networking/social-media.shtml

Joyce, S.P., *Guide to Twitter for Job Search.* Job Hunt, www.job-hunt.org/social-networking/twitter-job-search.shtml or via the short cut: https://tinyurl.com/k4qn5c5

Joyce, S.P., *Guide to Using Google for your Job Search.* Job Hunt, www. job-hunt.org/guides/google/using-google.shtml

Link Humans, *How People Use Facebook in Their Job Searches.* www. linkhumans.com/blog/using-facebook-job-search or via the short cut: https://tinyurl.com/k5e8zak

Morgan, H. *9 Tips to Leverage Facebook for a Successful Job Search.* Job Hunt, www.job-hunt.org/social-networking/facebook-job-search.shtml

Rose, A. (2016) *LinkedIn in 30 Minutes: How to Create a Rock-Solid LinkedIn Profile and Build Connections that Matter* (i30 Media, Boston, MA, USA, 2nd edn).

The Undercover Recruiter, *How to Use Facebook to Get Hired [5 Ways].* www.theundercoverrecruiter.com/5-ways-use-facebook-your-job-search/ or via the short cut: https://tinyurl.com/kovrekn

University of Buffalo, New York, School of Management, *How to Effectively use Social Media in your Job Search.* https://mgt.buffalo.edu/career-resource-center/students/networking/social-media/using.html or via the short cut: https://tinyurl.com/kryclth

These references are available for direct links on the eResource website.

8.9.1 Reference: eResources link for this book

For added resources and digital files related to this chapter:

Search: Routledge Text Books or go to: www.routledge.com/

Search window: type "Your Career", which will take you to the eResources for this book.

Or via the short cut: https://tinyurl.com/kyxnfaq

Then go to the Web References <TAB>, then the References <TAB>.

9 | Personal development

9.1 Introduction

Advancement in life (or career) is affected by what is happening inside us. Therefore, it is important that we understand ourselves. It can help make better choices; it can assist when facing challenges and aspects of job hunting that can be discouraging.

This chapter provides a brief overview of psychological techniques such as cognitive behavioural therapy (CBT); personality and aptitude assessment techniques such as Myers-Briggs Type Inventory® (MBTI®) and Strong Interest Inventory® (SII®).

Personal Development

Evaluating options and making choices is a part of job search preparation and hunting. These are choices relating to careers and jobs. Three decision-making tools are outlined. These will help you in job searching as well as in other areas of life. The aim is to help you weigh up career decisions, evaluate the better options and help you make choices.

9.2 Understanding yourself

9.2.1 What is going on inside?

Sometimes the biggest barrier to our advancement is what is going on inside us. Sometimes it is what is going on around us or background issues that affect how we conduct ourselves. It is usually easy to understand oneself in

94

terms of outward achievements. It is often harder to understand our inner selves. By understanding ourselves, we can make better career choices. Understanding yourself can also help handle the challenges of job searching and your reactions to things that happen. It is about understanding your thinking, your feelings and your behaviour.

9.2.2 Psychological techniques

Cognitive behavioural therapy (CBT) can be a useful technique. It recognises the power of the mind and provides techniques to deal with "negative" thinking. CBT is a method that helps us understand our behaviours. Burns (1999) popularised CBT in the 1980s with his bestselling book *Feeling Good*. CBT can be useful if you want to explore more deeply your thinking and behaviours.

Understanding Yourself: Psychological Techniques

Mindfulness is another technique. It allows us to note a negative thought and say "There is that thought again, but it will soon go." It does not attempt to stop negative thoughts or block them. It teaches us to accept them but not dwell on or adversely respond to them. It allows them to come and then pass on.

The way we think, guides the way we feel, which guides the way we behave.

If our thinking is sound, it has a positive influence on our lives, the way we feel and the way we behave. It affects our work relations and how we operate with others in our profession. Burns (1999), in his book *Feeling Good* helps us analyse our thinking. Is it OK? Is it off the mark (and possibly a root cause that we need to address within us)? Are there factors we need to examine within us to better handle the issues we face?

If our thinking is unsound it can drag us down. Our feelings become negative and our behaviour follows. This affects those around us – our family, friends and colleagues.

Examining yourself and being honest in your assessments can be valuable. The Myers-Briggs Type Indicator® (MBTI®) could be useful. It was designed to indicate psychological preferences in how people see the world and make decisions.

A short outline and a review of MBTI® from the Myers-Briggs organisation (www.myersbriggs.org) is included in the Appendix Resources 1: Myers-Briggs Type Indicator® (MBTI®).

STRONG Interest Inventory® (SII®) is another assessment tool. SII® assists in identifying your interests and preferences.

Personality and Career Assessment

You will need to decide if you want to explore these assessment tools further. There are online providers of MBTI® and SII® surveys. Some have also linked MBTI® and SII® to different careers and jobs. On completion of the surveys, you can request assessment reports on your interests, personality type, aptitude as well as links to different careers.

This may be useful if you are reviewing your career choices or exploring alternative job options.

The broad contents of these types of reports are briefly outlined in Appendix Resources 2: career assessment reports. It is intended as a short introduction to the types of online career assessment reports and services that are available.

See Career Assessment CPP: USA and Europe sites: www.cpp.com (USA) and www.opp.com (Europe), in the References at the end of this chapter.

Onetonline.com is a US career database which goes hand in hand with the MBTI® and SII® reports. This means that occupations are related to the assessment survey results (occupations that match your likes and dislikes and personality type) and can be found on this website. It includes information such as income, daily tasks, required education and so on.

Career guidance and evaluations are ideally done before you choose a course of study and career. They still can be useful after you have completed your course. They can help you choose particular career areas or alternate job areas by matching you personality and skills to different job types.

9.3 Decision-making tools

Decisions can often be the biggest barrier to progress or action. Trying to weigh up many different factors, some positive and some negative, in our minds can be hard. With many factors and options available it can be confusing or just too hard to decide. This means your progress is delayed.

Decision Making Tools

Decision-making tools are very useful. The issues are set out, the options brainstormed and then evaluated. This process separates decision making into smaller steps. It helps you see more clearly the options and possible impacts.

Three tools are covered:

- SWOT analysis: Appendix Personal Plan 7.

- Decision balance analysis: Appendix Personal Plan 8.

- Force field analysis: Appendix Personal Plan 9.

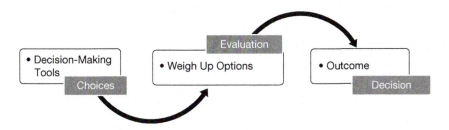

Proformas for the three tools are included in the Appendices.

To download the eResource digital versions, follow the instructions in the References at the end of this chapter.

Short forms are in the three Appendices Personal Plans 7, 8 and 9.

Longer forms with explanatory notes are in eResources in Decision Tools <TAB> <select tool>.

9.3.1 SWOT analysis

A tool that can be useful in making decisions and understanding challenges and barriers is SWOT analysis (strengths, weaknesses, opportunities and threats).

In job hunting, it can be useful to know your strengths and weaknesses. Understanding opportunities available and possible threats are also valuable. These can help you to build on your strengths and opportunities, and to address any weaknesses or threats as you seek a job.

It is a practical approach to addressing issues. You assess the situation under the four headings: strengths, weaknesses, opportunities and threats.

For each one, just write down bullet points or short phrases that relate to you and the situation. By brainstorming these headings you are addressing an issue in a systematic way. The positives – the strengths and opportunities – help you see your positive aspects. The negatives – weaknesses and threats – help you see things that may need attention. Understanding areas where you are not strong can be a positive. It can help you address these issues.

SWOT Analysis

By writing it down, it is easier to think it through. The alternative of letting all the aspects roll around in your mind is less likely to provide a clear picture and sound decision making.

A SWOT analysis framework is included. To download the eResource digital version, follow the instructions in the References at the end of the chapter. This is available in a short form in Appendix: Personal Plan 7 or in a longer form with explanation eResources Decision Tools <TAB> SWOT <TAB>.

Use it when you want to address an issue. Use it to help in your decision making.

See SWOT analysis origins in the References at the end of this chapter.

9.3.2 Decision balance analysis

This is another tool you can consider to help you evaluate situations and choices. Brainstorm options and complete the decision balance analysis pro forma. See Appendix Personal Plan 8: decision balance analysis.

The key steps are:

- Present situation (describe present situation or issue in short sentence or bullet points).

- Desired outcome (short sentence or bullet points).

- Possible or proposed options (short sentence or bullet points).

- Assessing the proposed option: if I choose this course of action ...

- Myself: the possible impacts for you (bullet points as your response).

  - *gains for self ...   *acceptable to you because ...
    *not acceptable to you because ...

  - *losses for self ...   *acceptable to you because ...
    *not acceptable to you because ...

If your option affects a significant other person such as husband, wife or partner, you can complete the possible impact statements for them.

If your option affects work colleagues (once in a job) you can complete the possible impact statements for them.

Decision Balance Analysis

9.3.2.1   Alternative options

The above decision making proforma can be used for other possible issues, potential solutions and good choices.

9.3.2.2   Evaluation

Use the responses you have made. The positive and negatives impacts (gains or losses) will let you assess more clearly the possible impacts of a particular option or course of action.

By setting it out clearly it will help you evaluate. It will assist you in your thinking and decision-making process as you complete the decision balance analysis.

Make the choice. It based on your best assessment at the time. It can always be changed later if you feel things have changed. You can rerun the decision balance process. The ultimate decision is yours, so just use these tools as an aid.

A decision balance proforma is included. To download the eResource digital version, follow the instructions in the References at the end of the chapter.

This is available in a short form in Appendix: Personal Plan 8: decision balance analysis or a longer form with explanation in eResources Decision Tools <TAB> Decision Balance <TAB>.

See decision balance analysis origins in the References at the end of this chapter.

9.3.3   Force field analysis

This is another tool somewhat similar to decision balance analysis. It approaches the issue to be addressed using different questions. Choose the decision-making tool that seems to best fit the challenge you are working through.

Force Field Analysis

- Describe the present situation or issue (short sentence or bullet points).
- Describe the desired outcome or solution (short sentence or bullet points).
- Assess the potential impact forces and the actions to maximise or minimise them.
- Assess the forces that help reach the desired outcome.
- Take actions to maximise these forces.
- Assess the forces that hinder reaching the desired outcome.

Actions to minimise these forces.

- Action plan: use the assessments above to prepare an action plan. Initially you may want to brainstorm possible actions. Then select the priority option.
- Commitment to action:
  - Identify the actions you will undertake in the coming week or fortnight, etc.
  - By putting it in writing it increases your likelihood of doing it.
  - This is part of your Personal Action plan to support your job hunting.

A force field analysis proforma is included. To download the eResource digital version, follow the instructions in the References at the end of the chapter. This is available in a short form in Appendix: Personal Plan 9: force field analysis, or a longer form with explanation in eResources Decision Tools <TAB> Force Field <TAB>.

9.4 Summary

This chapter introduced the value of seeking to understand yourself more. What are the things that motivate you? What things are you good at? A brief overview of psychological techniques such as CBT, personality and aptitude assessment techniques such as Myers-Briggs Type Inventory® (MBTI®) and Strong Interest Inventory® (SII®) have been provided. These are options you may consider. They can help us understand ourselves better and this helps in making job and career choices. They can also highlight personality characteristics, abilities and aptitudes. These are related to different job types.

The availability of online assessment services that link personality and aptitude assessment to jobs is a valuable resource that you can call on. Check out websites that offer these assessments if you feel it will help you in making job choices.

Three decision making tools have been outlined: SWOT analysis, decision balance analysis and force field analysis. Proformas are provided in the Appendices Resources.

Evaluating options and making choices is a part of job hunting. These are choices relating to careers and jobs. These tools can help you as you weigh up options and choices. They can help make sounder decisions.

In the next chapter you will identify your achievements. These are your "selling points". The chapter will help you to develop achievement statements for common job characteristics and personal attributes. These will be a valuable resource for your job search preparation.

9.5 References and further reading

9.5.1 Understanding yourself

Burns, D.D. (1999) *The Feeling Good Handbook*. (Harper Collins/William Morrow, New York, NY, USA).

Myers-Briggs Type Indicator® (MBTI)®. Developed by Katherine Cook Briggs and Isabel Briggs Myers.

The Myers & Briggs® Foundation. See: www.myersbriggs.org

STRONG Interest Inventory® (SII®). See: www.wikipedia.org for origins.

9.5.2 Career assessment

Career Assessment CPP: USA and Europe sites:
   www.cpp.com (USA)
   www.opp.com (Europe)

O *Net Online: Career database, see: www.Onetonline.com

9.5.3 Decision tools: origins

Cartwright, D. (1951) Foreword to the 1951 edition of *Field Theory in Social Science* by Kurt Lewin. Republished in *Resolving Social Conflicts & Field Theory in Social Science*. American Psychological Association, Washington, DC, 1997. Originally published by Harper & Row.

CPP: Strong Interest Inventory. Online career assessment example, www.cpp.com/en/strongproducts.aspx?pc=158 or via the short cut: https://tinyurl.com/ledvr3z

Decision balance analysis origins, see: https://en.wikipedia.org/wiki/Decisional_balance_sheet or via the short cut: https://tinyurl.com/mvv3qlp (In papers from 1959 onwards, Irving Janis and Leon Mann coined the phrase "decisional balance sheet".)

Force field analysis origins, see: https://en.wikipedia.org/wiki/Force-field_analysis or via the short cut: https://tinyurl.com/mz75jvp

Lewin, K. (1943) Defining the field at a given time. (*Psychological Review*, Vol. 50, Issue 3, pp. 292–310). Republished in *Resolving Social Conflicts & Field Theory in Social Science*, American Psychological Association, Washington, DC, 1997.

MBTI® Manual: A Guide to the Development and Use of the Myers-Briggs Type Indicator®, www.myersbriggs.org/my-mbti-personality-type/mbti-basics/ or via the short cut: https://tinyurl.com/2yhr4l

MTD Training (2013) *Personal Confidence & Motivation.* (Bookboon.com, London, UK).

SWOT analysis origins, see: https://en.wikipedia.org/wiki/SWOT_analysis or via the short cut: https://tinyurl.com/ls2ye7d

Wikipedia. Myers-Briggs, https://en.wikipedia.org/wiki/Myers%E2%80%93Briggs_Type_Indicator or via the short cut: https://tinyurl.com/odcrvvn

These references are available for direct links on the eResource website.

9.5.4 Reference: eResources link for this book

For added resources and digital files related to this chapter:

Search: Routledge Text Books or go to: www.routledge.com/

Search window: type "Your Career", which will take you to the eResources for this book.

Or via the short cut: https://tinyurl.com/kyxnfaq

Then go to either:

- Appendices <TAB> Personal Plan <TAB> (Appendices: Personal Plan); or
- Decision Tools <TAB> <then select tool>; or
- Web References <TAB> References <TAB>.

10 General Achievements
Developing your selling points

10.1 Introduction

In this chapter, the focus is on your achievements: how to recognise them and how to develop achievement statements. These will form a basis for your resume and interview responses.

Initially, the main achievements or job criteria that are common to most jobs are identified: teamwork, communication, people skills, quality, commitment, timeliness and customer service.

As part of your Personal Plan, you will develop your achievement statements for each of these.

In addition, other skills and achievements will be identified: word processing, spreadsheets, computer skills, software tools, problem solving skills, analysis skills and self-motivation.

Corresponding achievement statements will be created.

Achievements Statements | Developing Your Selling Points

10.2 General Achievements: developing your selling points

General Achievements

Recognising your achievements and relating them to a job criterion is important preparation for job applications. In this chapter, we cover achievements that are common to most jobs. They can be prepared prior to having a specific job specification. We have called them General Achievements. In the next chapter you will cover achievements that relate to specific jobs. These have been called Achievements Extended.

For both of these achievements, the Appendix: Personal Plan will assist you in identifying them and describing them. This is valuable for your later Foundation Resume and as preparation for interviews.

The initial challenge many young graduates face is how to respond to questions regarding their achievements. They may feel they do not have anything to report. They are seeking a job to build an achievements profile. Job criteria and prospective questions about your achievements may seem to be a formidable aspect. What do you put in your resume if you are a new graduate? What do you say in the interview?

Through the guidance in this book and your Personal Plan, you will address this challenge. It will draw on your wider life: university, part-time work, volunteer activities, sporting participation and community involvement.

Your confidence in your ability to respond to job skills criteria will lift as you prepare your Personal Plan 10: General Achievements. You will be surprised that you have already been developing the common skills of many jobs.

10.2.1 Achievements: recognise them

Achievements: Recognise Them

First, learn to recognise your achievements in areas such as:

- Teamwork: this comes from group activities and joint projects.

- Quality: your approach to high-quality output in assignments and projects.

- Commitment: what you have been doing to complete your degree and course assignments.

- Timeliness: meeting assignment deadlines is one aspect.

- People skills: working with others on team projects.

- Communication: written and verbal skills you have developed through your course.

- Customer service: ways to relate to people to whom you provide a service.

10.2.2   Achievements: how to develop them

Through your university course you will have developed some of these achievements (e.g. communication skills or teamwork skills in group projects).

Through other outside activities you may have developed further achievements. It may be via part-time work, volunteering activities, sporting or special interest roles you have had.

Other ways to develop skills include: reading books on the topic (e.g. personal communications) or taking a personal development course (e.g. relationship skills if this is important for your career area).

As you complete your Personal Plan, you will be able to respond to questions on these skills.

There are other skills, such as word processing, spreadsheets and Internet use. If you feel you are weak in any of these criteria, you may need to further build your skills. You can do a short course. Often these are available online. They will enhance your marketability for a job. It will also show the interview panel (and via your resume) that you have a commitment to grow and develop professionally.

In some skill criteria you may not have specific achievements to present. This can be overcome by outlining your values on these criteria. Employers recognise that new graduates will not have experience in all criteria. What they are looking for is your potential to develop, your interest and commitment to this area.

For example, if the skill topic is quality, your response may be:

- I take a quality approach to all things that I undertake.

- I always check my work before submitting it, to guarantee high quality.

● I seek to produce quality results in my university subjects, part-time work or other activities.

10.2.3   How to create achievement statements

Create Achievement Statements

This will involve an investment of your time to do this. You will brainstorm your achievements for each topic, refine these into succinct and short statements, and edit them so they are well expressed.

For each achievement criteria you will prepare two or three short achievement statements; each should be just one or two lines to keep it brief. If you cannot think of actual examples, then add in your value statement (see quality example above).

Examples of achievement statements are covered in Appendix Resources 3: general achievement examples.

10.3   Teamwork

This is about how we work with others. Most projects involve a combination of different team members' skills. Each team member provides a contribution. Your skills in working with others – as a team member – are important.

Teamwork

Some examples of a teamwork achievement statement are:

● My teamwork skills were initially developed during my employment at (company). During work experience, I recognise the value of building team skills.

● During my university studies, I worked well in group project assignments, where I often acted as the coordinator.

10.4 Communication skills

Communication is a key part of all jobs. It ranges from verbal to written communication. In addition, body language, that is, non-verbal messages, tone and speaking style, is a crucial and major aspect of any interpersonal communication. It is a valuable skill to understand and develop. Your body language is a key part of the way you effectively communicate with others. It also helps you understand what others may really be saying, or not saying.

We will cover this further in Chapter 17: Interviews.

Are you able to express issues clearly to other team members? Can you prepare a written proposal that clearly communicates your objective? If the reader or person listening (manager, team member or clients) does not understand what you are communicating, then your efforts have been wasted. It is important to grow yourself personally in the area of communication. Practice your verbal skills, including presentations.

Communication

Progressively enhance your written skills. Learn ways of improving yourself and be willing to ask others for constructive feedback. Take their advice on board and do not react defensively, but use it to improve. At the job preparation stage, you are seeking to identify your communication skills.

An example of a communication skills achievement statement is:

- My written communication skills have developed during my university course via assignments and my thesis.

- My verbal skills are at a high level, from having given many presentations during my studies.

- My communication – interpersonal and verbal skills – are at a high level. I always seek to improve these. I recognise their importance for good work operations.

10.5 People skills

People are a key ingredient in all organisations. They involve teams, the technical and professional people, the support staff, through to management. Development of your people skills is a valuable commodity; it will underpin your career.

A narrow approach is to think that a job is purely about technical or professional knowledge. This knowledge, without appropriate people skills, can be ineffective. The aim is to get a good balance between knowledge, technical solutions and interpersonal relations. Given the choice between high knowledge skills combined with poor people skills versus moderate knowledge skills combined with good people skills, many managers and interview panels will opt for the latter. People skills are important. Organisations need staff who have good people skills and are able to work with other team members, supervisors and clients. This results in smoother operations and avoids potential conflict and disruption. It is important to keep developing your people skills.

People Skills

An example of a people skills achievement statement is:

- My interpersonal skills are well developed. This will be important in interacting with a wide range of people within the organisation and possibly external clients.
- My personal characteristics include: easy to get on with and cooperative. This helps build good relations with other team members and managers.
- As a good listener, my interpersonal skills are appreciated in most meetings and activities I have been involved in.

10.6 Quality

Quality is an important part of all jobs. None of us value poor quality work. Other people and clients, who receive work outputs from a professional group or organisation, assume that they will be receiving professional quality products and services. Quality should be part of all organisations' value systems. This applies to private businesses and government organisations. Developing a quality ethos is valuable – it will benefit you and your employer.

One of the great challenges all professions and businesses face is the balance of quality and fitness for purpose. If your project involves developing a product or service, your approach could be to contribute a "Rolls Royce" solution that is of exceptional quality. Yet this may not be what the client needs. They may just require something practical and affordable that fits the purpose. Excessive quality is not a desired or required option in this case. Your challenge will be to recognise from the client's brief or manager's specifications or project requirements, what is the appropriate quality level. This is not about poor quality; it is about quality that is fit for purpose. This is what you are aiming for and this represents true professionalism. An ability to adapt the quality to the specifications, the time available and the budget is a valuable skill. Together they enable a cost-effective, practical solution that meets the client's needs, timeframe and available funds.

An example of a quality achievement statement is:

- I take pride in completing quality work and projects.
- I always check the quality of my work before submitting it to my supervisor.
- I have always sought to produce quality results in my university subjects and part-time work.
- I have an understanding of the quality assurance standards for ... (e.g. road design).

10.7 Commitment

The energy and enthusiasm that you can bring to a potential new job or tasks reflects commitment. It is about your desire to devote your time and energy to the task required. Employers prefer someone who is committed over a person with skills but limited commitment. This can be sensed during an interview by the way you may respond as well as the ways you have undertaken projects in the past. If a tender application for a work project needs extra effort or an added time commitment, will a potential employer feel that you will be there with the rest of the team? Learn how to be committed and show it in your job resume and interviews.

Commitment

An example of a commitment achievement statement is:

- Completion of a university degree and additional subjects (list major relevant ones) have reflected a commitment to the way I operate.
- As member of the university's Special Events Committee, I always showed my commitment by going the extra mile to ensure the event was on time and properly planned.
- My part-time employment over the past four years at (company) has required both reliability and commitment. I have met and exceeded the requirements of my employer.

10.8 Timeliness

This is about delivering a product or service on time. It concerns meeting an agreed delivery date. It helps a customer if all the components are delivered as agreed and expected. Any delay that you may be part of can have an adverse roll-on effect and cost impacts. It can lead to the loss of your customer's confidence in your organisation. Poor timeliness leads to delays in projects.

At times, activities outside your control can lead to potential time delays. Your challenge is to provide information to your client as early as possible about any potential delays. Customers and managers appreciate this. It is not about excuses. It is about explaining the factors and other external issues that may influence the delivery of the project. If you are open at an early stage, it helps retain clients when timeliness becomes an issue. Last minute excuses about non-delivery can result in your clients moving elsewhere.

Timeliness

An example of a timeliness achievement statement is:

- I value timeliness – I seek to meet deadlines and be reliable in my time schedules involving others.

- I believe I have well-developed attitudes to promptness and meeting agreed timeframes.

- I pride myself on providing the best quality service, within the time specified.

10.9 Customer service

This is a key area in all jobs and professions. It is not just for those involved face-to-face with external or "buying" customers. In its broadest sense, a customer is someone to whom you provide a service. It may be someone in your team. You may be providing a professional service to them as part of a wider project; it may be another work unit or it could be your supervisor. The concept is: if you are not dealing directly in providing customer service to an external client, you are providing support and customer service to other team members or managers, who interact directly with customers.

Customer service is not restricted to commercial business organisations. It applies equally to government organisations and non-government organisations. Each of these needs to demonstrate customer service to continue to retain value and the confidence of the organisation. Probably the largest failure in government units is in this area.

Customer Service

An example of a customer service achievement statement is:

- Client service skills have been developed in my part-time work at (employer), which involves my relating to and serving customers. I recognise its importance and have developed skills in customer service.

- Working in the university's bookshop for three years, I have increased my customer service skills.

10.10 Personal Plan: main general achievements

Examples of General Achievement statements are in the Appendix Resources 3: general achievement examples. To download the eResource digital Appendices: Personal Plan, follow the instructions in the References at the end of the chapter. Now commence your Appendix Personal Plan 10: general achievements.

This covers the main general criteria: teamwork, communication, people skills, quality, commitment, timeliness and customer service. It will take time and effort to work through these. It is a great investment of your time. They become a valuable resource for responding to interview questions. Selected ones will be used in your Foundation Resume (and later Targeted Resume) where they are significant for the job.

So, have you completed these seven key achievements in your Personal Plan? Make sure you keep your Personal Plan sections up to date. You will be surprised to see afterwards how much you have already achieved before applying for your first job!

10.11 Other skills

10.11.1 Word processing and spreadsheets

Many jobs involve tools such as word processing and spreadsheets or the Internet. It is worthwhile outlining your achievements and skills.

Word Processing

For example:

- Word processing – I have developed skills in using Word.
- I am adept at using spreadsheets, especially Excel, which I used extensively for my various assignments at university.

10.11.2   Computer and Internet

Many jobs require general computing and Internet skills. It is worthwhile outlining your achievements and skills.

Computer and Internet

For example:

- Computer and Internet skills: I have a good level of proficiency using all types of digital media, personal computers, tablets, smart phones, as well as a good ability to use the Internet.
- I am familiar with Apple, Android and Microsoft systems.

10.11.3   Software tools

For many jobs, computer software tools may be a key part of the work. Identify any computer tools that are essential or widely used in your profession. For example, if you are an architect or engineer then CAD (computer aided design) software is important.

Software Tools

Identify your skills in any particular software packages. For example:

- CAD software: I have completed a course in (name) CAD system design.
- CAD software: I have used CAD software for university projects and my skills are growing.
- I have experience in using image processing and GIS software.
- I am able to programme in (name) language(s).

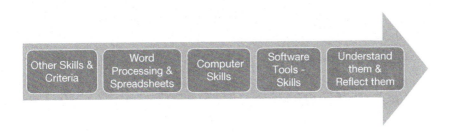

10.12 Personal Plan: other skills

We have outlined word processing, spreadsheets, computer and Internet use skills. Examples of achievement statements for these are in Appendix Resources 3: general achievement examples.

Now commence your Personal Plan: general achievements for these other skills. See Appendix Personal Plan 10: general achievements.

Once you have completed this part of your Personal Plan you will have identified and written short achievement statements about these "other skills and criteria" described above.

Now we will go on to identify your personal achievements.

10.13 Personal achievements

Personal Achievements

10.13.1 Problem solving and analysis

These are important in certain professions. If so, you should develop achievement statements that reflect your ability or potential.

Problem Solving and Analysis

For example:

- Problem solving and analysis: I have developed problem solving and analysis skills during my university course.

- I enjoy the challenge of solving problems and value my ability to critically analyse issues and develop solutions.

- My studies involved solving complex problems. This really stimulates me.

10.13.2 *Self-motivation*

Employers value this quality. They seek employees who do not need step-by-step direction, but are motivated to do what is required. Self-motivated employees display energy and enthusiasm. Plus, they can tackle tasks or problems as they are self-motivated to deliver an outcome.

Self-Motivation

For example:

- Self-motivation: I am motivated to complete assigned tasks.

- Self-motivation: once I am given a task to undertake, I have the energy and enthusiasm to complete it.

- As soon as I understand what has to be done, I am extremely motivated to produce the best result possible.

- I am good at taking the initiative to carry out new tasks.

10.14 Personal Plan: personal skills

Examples of achievement statements for these are in: Appendix Resources 3: General Achievement examples. See Appendix Personal Plan 10: general achievements to develop statements for these personal skills (problem solving and analysis; self-motivation).

Now complete your Personal Plan: general achievements.

Your achievements are now really starting to look impressive!

In the next chapter, we develop your achievement statements further by adding more extended achievements relating especially to your profession and the job you are applying for.

10.15 Further information on achievement statements

Firestone's (2014) *Ultimate Guide to Job Interview – Answers* is a valuable and informative book on the key aspects of interviews for jobs and interview preparation. A summary of key points has been included in the Appendix Resources 9: interviews: expert's advice.

In it, the author uses the term "behavioral competencies". These are similar to "achievements" as described in this book. In this book, we have focused on seven general achievements (competencies) that are common to most jobs: teamwork, communication, people skills, quality, commitment, timeliness and customer service.

In this book, each achievement (related to job criteria) is converted to two or three achievement statements with each one being one to two short lines or a few short bullet points.

Firestone (2014) identifies 40 competencies. They are grouped in themes that can relate to interview question areas. He uses SOARL as an acronym to develop the achievement statements. This represents a situation/objective/action/results/ learning approach.

This is another way to create your achievement statements.

With both approaches, you have recognised your achievements for key themes (such as teamwork), and created achievement statements for each one. These will be used later for your resume, job application and interview responses.

10.16 Summary

At the conclusion of this chapter and the completion of your Personal Plan: general achievements, you will have made significant progress. It takes some time to brainstorm, prepare and edit each achievement statement. It is a great investment. It embeds your achievements into your memory and makes it easy for you to recall them at short notice during an interview.

This chapter has addressed the general achievements in three broad groups:

● Seven common achievement areas (such as teamwork, communication, etc.).

- Other skills (such as computer skills, word processing, etc.).

- Personal skills (such as problem solving or self-motivation).

For each achievement topic you will have two to three bullet points; each will be a short one or two line sentence that highlights your achievements. Once completed they can readily be:

- included in your resume (if especially relevant to the job); and

- used in interviews for your responses on a topic (e.g. teamwork).

They are a valuable resource of your achievements that you can easily draw on in job applications.

At the end of the process you may surprise yourself with your achievements. These will come from your university course and various other areas of your life. This will boost your confidence as you prepare job applications and undertake job interviews.

Congratulations, you have made some major steps forward. You have recognised your general achievements. You have an understanding of some typical job criteria as well as the skills and achievements required.

In the next chapter, you develop Achievements Extended statements. These will be more related to specific careers and job requirements.

10.17   References and further reading

Arruda, W. and Dixson, K. (2007) *Career Distinction: Stand Out by Building Your Brand.* (Wiley Publishers, Hoboken, NJ, USA).

Firestone, B. (2014) *Ultimate Guide to Job Interview – Answers.* (Success Patterns, Santa Monica, CA, 7th edn).

Pollak, L. (2012) *Getting from College to Career: Your Essential Guide to Succeeding in the Real World.* (Harper Business, New York, NY, USA, rev. edn).

Savage, R.D. (1974) Personality and achievement in higher education professional training. (*Educational Review*, Vol. 27, Issue 1, pp. 3–15).

Sweeny, J. (2014) *Moving the Needle: Get Clear, Get Free, and Get Going in Your Career, Business and Life*. (Wiley Publishers, Hoboken, NJ, USA).

10.17.1 Reference: eResources link for this book

For added resources and digital files related to this chapter:

Search: Routledge Text Books or go to: www.routledge.com/

Search window: type "Your Career", which will take you to the eResources for this book.

Or via the short cut: https://tinyurl.com/kyxnfaq

Then go to either:

- Appendices <TAB> . . . Personal Plan <TAB> (Appendices: Personal Plan); or
- Appendices <TAB> Resources <TAB> (Appendices: Resources); or
- Web References <TAB> References <TAB>.

11 Achievements Extended
Further selling points

11.1 Introduction

In this chapter the focus is on your Achievements Extended. These relate to specific careers and jobs. The aim is to develop further selling points that you can use for your resume, job applications and interviews. These will help you market yourself.

In the previous chapter, the attention was on General Achievements. These were ones common to most jobs: teamwork, communication skills, people skill, quality, commitment, timeliness and customer service.

Achievement statements are developed next for your selected career and profession.

They can be further developed for specific job criteria. The chapter will show how to recognise them and develop them in your Personal Plan: Achievements Extended.

Examples of extended achievement statements are provided in Appendix Resources 4: Achievements Extended examples.

These achievement statements will be a valuable resource for your resume and interview preparation.

Recognising Your Achievements ... Building Your Selling Points

11.2 Achievements Extended

11.2.1 Overview

Each profession and job will have specific achievement criteria. These are outlined in job specifications. What do you put in your resume if you are a new graduate? What do you say in the interview?

The challenge for new graduates is how to address these criteria, particularly if you have little or no work experience. We will help you to respond to these achievement criteria and questions.

Extended Achievements

Through this chapter and its Personal Plan, you will recognise and describe your extended achievements. These will be short bullet point style statements that you can easily add to a job application or use in an interview.

11.2.2 Achievements: recognise them

Through your university course and life you may have developed a number of these extended achievements. It may be via part-time work while at university, volunteer work or possibly sporting and special interest roles you have had. The challenge is to recognise them and then incorporate them into your resume and interview responses. Use them to help win a job.

Achievements: Recognise Them

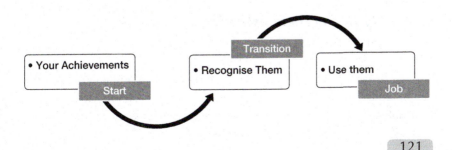

11.2.3   Extended achievements: how to develop them

The range of extended skills and achievements can be developed through activities such as:

- Part-time employment in your chosen career.

- Part-time employment in any other field.

- Volunteer work: as you help others (perhaps a charity organisation, community group or sporting body) you are developing your own skills. It helps both the organisation and yourself.

- Reading books on any new skills you feel weak in and wish to develop further.

- Taking a personal development course, perhaps in communication skills, for example.

In some skill criteria, you may not have specific achievements to present. This can be overcome by outlining your values on these criteria or skills. Employers recognise that new graduates will not have experience in all criteria. What they are looking for is your potential to develop, your interest and commitment to this area.

For example if the skill topic is quality, your response may be:

- I take a quality approach to all tasks that are undertaken.

- I seek to produce quality results in (my university subjects and part-time work).

11.2.4   How to create extended achievement statements

This will involve an investment of your time to do this. You will brainstorm your extended achievements for each topic, refine these into succinct and short statements, and edit them so they are well expressed.

For each achievement, you will come up with one to three short achievement statements; they should each be one or two lines in order to keep it brief. If you cannot think of actual examples, then add in your value statement (see quality example above).

Create Achievement Statements

11.3 Profession-specific achievements

Professional requirements are reflected in the job criteria. For example, if your career is in architecture, then visual presentation and graphics skills are relevant. If it is in engineering, then engineering design and problem-solving skills are relevant.

Job specifications and criteria can help you identify these. Speak to a mentor or senior professional in the area to help you identify them. You will shortly develop your professional achievement statements, as part of your Personal Plan: Achievements Extended.

Profession-Specific Achievements

For example, a pharmacist will require skills that convert a customer's request or medical condition into the most appropriate medication.

For example:

- Assessing customers' medicinal needs – I believe it is important to develop skills to convert customers' needs to the most appropriate medication; I have sought to develop this skill further in my practical training.

11.4 Personal Plan: profession-specific

Examples of extended achievement statements are covered in Appendix Resources 4: Achievements Extended examples. To download the eRe-source digital Appendices: Personal Plan, follow the instructions in the References at the end of the chapter. Now commence your Appendix Personal Plan 11: Achievements Extended. This covers profession-specific achievements. Identify them as a single one-line heading. Then develop your response as short bullet points (of one to three lines maximum).

11.5 Job-specific achievements

Besides the more general professional requirements, some jobs have job specific ones. It is important to read each job criteria in detail. Do not just use a standard job application resume for all job applications. It is important to address each criterion, one by one. Adapt your resume and fine tune it for different job criteria.

Job-Specific Achievements

Carefully read the job selection criteria. Identify any particular specific requirements. Develop achievement statements or value statements for them. These will be two or three bullet points, each having just one or two lines to reflect your achievements or value system. For example, if an engineering job requires workplace health and safety skills, your achievement statement may be:

● Workplace health and safety skills: I have completed a health and safety module for engineering sites. I recognise this is an important area to continue to develop further.

This preparation will flow into your thoughts and memory. Not only is it available for the job application and resume, it is a valuable resource to draw on if questions arise during your interview.

Job Criteria: Achievements ▷ Recognise them ▷ Reflect them in your application

11.6 Personal Plan: job-specific

Examples of these achievement statements are covered in Appendix Resources 4: Achievements Extended examples. Now commence your Appendix Personal Plan 11: Achievements Extended (for job-specific criteria). Identify them as a single one-line heading. Then develop your response as short bullet points (of one to four lines).

11.7 Personal achievements

Your personal achievements may help you stand out.

Many potential new jobs involve many applicants. Each applicant is trying to be selected for an interview. Part of your aim in your job application, cover letter and resume, is to stand out. If there are extra factors that make you a little bit different to others, and if these are relevant to the job, it is worthwhile developing achievement statements for them.

For example, if you had a role as a secretary of a volunteer or sporting body, then this may be a valuable skill in the job you are seeking. It will reflect an ability to manage meetings and organisational demands or coordinate activities.

Personal Achievements

For example, your personal achievement statement might be:

- Secretarial and coordination skills: in my role as secretary of (...) I have developed skills in managing meetings, completing organisational demands and coordinating the activities of other members of the organisation.

Another example might be if you do volunteer work in an aged care facility and your profession is in the healthcare area, in which case you may want to highlight this achievement:

- Aged care skills: in my voluntary capacity assisting at (...) I have developed an ability to relate to aged patients and assist them.

These may be added skills and achievements from other activities you have done. This could include, perhaps, a role in a sporting organisation or volunteer activities.

11.8 Personal Plan: personal achievements

Examples of personal achievements are covered in Appendix Resources 4: Achievements Extended examples. Continue with Appendix Personal Plan 11: Achievements Extended (for personal achievements). Identify them as a single one-line heading. Then develop your response as short bullet points (of one to four lines).

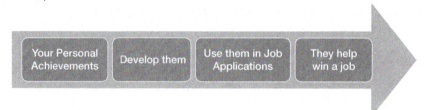

11.9 Summary

Recognised and Developed Extended Achievement Statements

This chapter has shown you how to recognise and develop extended achievement statements.

You have developed these for your profession and for specific job criteria. In addition, you may have covered some extra personal factors that make you stand out.

It takes some time to brainstorm, prepare and edit each achievement statement. It is a great investment. It embeds your achievements into your memory and makes it easy for you to recall them at short notice during an interview. Type them up. Keep them as an easily accessible and valuable resource.

At the end of the process you may surprise yourself with your achievements. These will come from your university course and various other areas of your life. This will boost your confidence as you prepare job applications. They will be useful as you prepare for job interviews.

Congratulations, you have made some major steps forward. Your Personal Plan 11: Achievements Extended can provide valuable inputs for your Foundation Resume.

In the next chapters, your will use your General Achievements and Achievements Extended to prepare your Foundation Resume.

11.10   References and further reading

Hill, N. (2011) *The 17 Principles of Personal Achievement.* (A Plume Book, New York, NY, USA, audio-CD edn).

Pollak, L. (2012) *Getting from College to Career: Your Essential Guide to Succeeding in the Real World.* (Harper Business, New York, NY, USA, rev. edn).

Stapleton, S., 7 keys to describe your achievements – pro style, Simon-Stapleton.com. See: www.simonstapelton.com/wordpress/2009/08/10/7-keys-to-describe-your-achievements/ or via the short cut: https://tinyurl.com/lrbp9w2

Tracy, B. (1997) *Great Little Book on Personal Achievement.* (Successories, Career Press, Wayne, NJ, USA).

What are some examples of personal achievements? See: www.reference.com/business-finance/examples-personal-achievements-107dda84830d006e or via the short cut: https://tinyurl.com/mx49yut

11.10.1   Reference: eResources link for this book

For added resources and digital files related to this chapter:

Search: Routledge Text Books or go to: www.routledge.com/

Search window: type "Your Career", which will take you to the eResources for this book.

Or via the short cut: https://tinyurl.com/kyxnfaq

Then go to either:

- Appendices <TAB> Personal Plan <TAB> (Appendices: Personal Plan); or

- Appendices <TAB> Resources <TAB> (Appendices: Resources).

Follow the download instructions. Then save it to a working folder on your PC.

Preparing your Foundation Resume

Stage 1

12.1 Introduction

In different countries and regions there are different words used to describe your personal profile, education, skills and abilities for a position. In some countries it is resume; in others it is curriculum vitae or CV for short. In some such as the USA, resume is often used for a job application, whereas curriculum vitae refers to a more academic resume.

We have adopted the standard term resume. As we progress through the stages of developing your resume, we have used the Foundation Resume to indicate a base document containing a wide range of your skills and abilities.

This chapter builds on the achievements that you have started to develop in the preceding chapters and in your Personal Plan.

In Appendix Personal Plan 10: General Achievements you have created short statements that reflect your achievements. In Appendix Personal Plan 11: Achievements Extended you have created short statements that reflect your achievements in relation to a career and specific job criteria. Both these documents are a valuable resource. They are useful as you prepare your Foundation Resume and later will be useful in preparing for interviews.

Your Foundation Resume will be developed in two stages. This chapter is stage 1. It provides guidance on presentation techniques to prepare your resume and to make it stand out. The aim is for it to be easily read. Options are given for content, order and sample resumes.

In this chapter's Personal Plan you will prepare the outline (key points) for your Foundation Resume. This means you can apply the advice in the book to your job preparation. Remember the concept behind the Foundation Resume is a resource of your achievements.

In the next chapter, you will extend it so it relates to a specific job. In Chapter 15 of the book, your Foundation Resume will be modified to become your selected country and the specific job. It will be become your Targeted Resume, a brief one- to two-page document that accompanies your job application.

12.2   Resume development stages: overview

Resume Development Stages

To provide an overview of the whole process, the book takes you through:

- Personal Plan: Use the Personal Plan to reflect your work experience, abilities and education. You progressively build up your achievements as concise statements. It allows you to focus on one issue at a time with a step-by-step approach.

- Foundation Resume: Compile your Personal Plan outputs into a resume. This is much more than a job application resume. It contains a large amount of concise information on your experience, qualifications, abilities and so on. It is also a resource of information to draw on for job interviews. We recommend that you do this in a digital format using the template you select.

- Targeted Resume: Later, draw on your Foundation Resume to prepare your shorter job application resume. It will be in your selected country format and relate to a specific job and its criteria. This will be covered later in Chapter 15: Preparing your targeted resume.

Personal Plan: Your Achievements via Appendices	➡	Foundation Resume: Your Achievements Resource	➡	Targeted Resume: For Your Job Application

In this chapter and the next, you are preparing via your Personal Plan, the concise statements that will go into your Foundation Resume.

12.3 Select Foundation Resume template

It is recommended that you select a template for your Foundation Resume. This way you can start compiling your achievements into a resume format. It is a resource of your abilities, education and work experience. It is a digital document.

The options are:

● Use one of the resume examples in this book:

Appendix Resources 5: Foundation Resume Example One; or

Appendix Resources 6: Foundation Resume Example Two.

● Use a free resume template. These are available from many university websites and career advice centres; or

● Use a resume template from a job search agency (these may be free or you may be required to pay for added services such as resume preparation, resume checking or job search assistance); or

● Use a free resume template from YouExec. Further information follows in the next section.

The resume templates above can be downloaded from the book's eResource website. See the eResource link in the References at end of this chapter.

| Foundation Resume Template: Options | Appendices Resources 5 & 6: Resume Options | University / Career Centre: Resume Templates | Job Search Agency: Resume Templates | YouExec: Free Resume Templates |

12.4 Free digital resume template: YouExec

Free Digital Resume Template

The following section outlines one option to access a digital resume template.

YouExec is a US career, business and professional development organisation. It essentially operates via volunteer contributions. Its mission is career development for professionals. It shares advice and resources on careers and business. These are valuable resources and are free. In particular, they provide free access to downloadable resume/CV templates. These are designed for different career situations. They range from internal resumes (within the same organisation), mid-career resumes to new graduates resumes.

The subscription to the free weekly newsletter provides updates about career developments, business and new insights. You can unsubscribe at any time.

Alternatively, users can choose to subscribe to "Plus", which costs US$5/month and provides access to a greater range of professional development and career resources. You can unsubscribe at any time from "Plus". Paid subscriptions go to maintain the organisation, the website, personal development resources and to commission new career resources. They provide links to the top 200 best business books and their summaries.

See YouExec, *Resume Templates and Other Career Resources*, in the References at the end of this chapter.

12.4.1 Resume template

YouExec's "Ultimate Resource Kit" provides access to free career development information and downloadable resources. In particular, they have two templates for resumes/CVs for new graduates. It is accessible via the YouExec website.

Go to: www.youexec.com
Select either:

- "Start Now": takes you to start up for links to YouExec resources; or
- "Subscribe": free subscription to weekly newsletter on career development, business insights and professional development.

Both require you to enter your email address.

To access the free "Ultimate Resource Kit" where you can select and download a resume template for new graduates, go to: www.youexec.com/ultimate-resume

This will allow you to access the "Ultimate Resume Kit". You will need to enter your email so they can send you a download link for resume templates. Click "Subscribe". There is no charge.

You will receive a welcome email titled: welcome + resume kit verification. Then an email follows shortly with your personalised download link.

In the email titled: welcome + resume kit download, select "Get Free Resume Kit".

Download the resume link; the one for new graduates is Unidade, light blue option (or dark blue option, which is more for internal job applications). Select an option and download, then save this template for your resume development.

12.4.2 Subscription services

Signing up to YouExec's "Plus" service costs US$5/month. This provides access to premium resources – a wider range of career development, professional resources and business insights. Users can unsubscribe at any time.

The above free resume material (from YouExec) can be accessed via the book's eResource webpage. See the References: eResources link at the end of this chapter.

12.5 Preparing your Foundation Resume

12.5.1 Your aims

Aims

- Prepare, draft and edit a professional resume (clear, well presented and highlighting your capabilities).

- Outline your personal attributes, qualifications, achievements and experience.

- Use good visual presentation techniques (space, selected bullet points and layout). Provide a visually attractive document that is easy to read or scan read.

- Make you stand out as a potential candidate.

- Understand the needs of employers and interview panels, and tailor your presentation to assist them.

For many jobs, there are many applications. This can involve a lot of time for the manager and interview panel. They all have other responsibilities and this can become an additional load. Your approach should be to make their job easier.

12.5.2   Resume: contents and order

There are a number of common elements in a good resume. The presentation and layout can vary between countries. Although the substantial material is nearly always the same, you may need to adapt the presentation to the context, culture and norms for your country.

Different options are presented below on the order of the resume material. Choose a format that you feel best shows your achievements and matches the job criteria. Chapter 15 will take you through adapting your Foundation Resume to a particular country and common resume layout.

12.5.3   Resume contents: option one

Resume: Option One

- Header with a name – visually attractive.
- Career goals.
- Overview of skills and capabilities.
  The following will be a short summary via a few bullet points for each item:

  o   Overview: to relate you personally to the job.

  o   Key skills: to relate you to the key skills required for the job.

  o   Personal characteristics: to relate your characteristics to the job.

  o   Interests and activities: to show your wider activities and abilities.

These are intended to be an easily scan read summary. It aims to help the manager or interview panel quickly see how you relate to the job. After all, you are trying to make their job easier.

- General skills.
  Depending on the nature of your job, these can include skills that are often common across jobs. They may include teamwork, communication, people skills, quality, commitment, timeliness and customer service (use short sentences or bullet points for the relevant ones).

- Job-specific skills.
  These relate to the particular job or to organisation specific job criteria (use short sentence or bullet points for each one).

- Key qualifications.
  - University qualifications.
  - Other qualifications.
  - Other courses and achievements.

- Employment experience.
  This can be specific employment-related experience as well as more general work experience.
  The latter can show you have a range of experiences and work skills. Work experience.
  - Year and organisation.
  - Short sentence about your role and achievements.

- Referees.
  - Contact names, telephone numbers and email addresses (or say "Can be supplied on request").
    Normally, you will need to provide at least three names of referees to include in your resume. If the potential employer is interested in your resume, they may contact some of these referees to vouch for you and to provide some further background about you. So, before you insert their names on your resume, you should have contacted them to ask if they would be willing to act as a referee if requested and send them a copy of your resume, plus any relevant information about the specific job you are applying for, as well as any information you have about the organisation (e.g. the company's website).

○ Some companies and organisations ask you to submit your references together with your resume. In that case, you need to ask your referees to write a more general reference for you. It is best to keep your submitted materials to the basics, such as a good cover letter and your resume.

For an employer, it is much easier to email or phone your referees, once you have reached the interview stage.

● Personal details.

○ Name: make sure it is clear which is your family name and which is your first name. If there is any possible confusion, put your family name in bold uppercase letters and your first name in lower case letters.

○ Birth year: note in some countries they will not ask you for your age or date of birth, as this is against the country's discrimination laws. They are not allowed to select the successful applicant on the basis of age, sex, religion or other personal characteristics. If it is not asked for in the job vacancy announcement, then do not provide it.

○ Date of birth: (see above comment).

○ Gender: (see above comment). Bear in mind that in many Western countries, there is a government policy that if there are two applicants with equal ability and suitability for a particular job, then the female candidate must be selected, because of gender inequality in certain professions.

○ Address: give your full postal address with postal/zip code. Note that many employers do not prefer post office box numbers (PO box) in an address, but prefer a physical street location.

○ Phone: give your home telephone number, your mobile or cell phone number, and if already in a temporary job, your work number.

○ Email address: give your personal email address.

For an example of this type of resume, see Appendix Resources 5: Foundation Resume example 1 or download the digital version from the book's eResource website.

See the References: eResource link at the end of the chapter.

Follow links to the Appendices: Resources or Templates <TAB> Resumes/CVs <TAB>.

12.5.4 Resume contents: option two

Resume: Option Two

- Resume header with your name.

- Personal information overview.
  This is an overview of your tertiary qualification, goals, professional skills, general skills and personal characteristics. It should be a summary to provide an easy to read outline of the resume. The details follow later in the resume.
  - o University qualification overview: to show degree, university and any majors.
  - o Goals: your personal goals related to the job or career area.
  - o Profession skills overview: your link to the main criteria.
  - o General skills overview: select a couple of main general skills that relate to the job requirements.
  - o Personal characteristics: to relate your characteristics to the job.

- Qualifications.
  - o University qualifications.
  - o Other qualifications.
  - o Other courses and achievements.

- Work experience.
  This can be specific employment-related experience as well as more general work experience. The latter can show you have a range of experiences and work skills.
  - o Year/organisation.
  - o Short sentence about your role and achievements.

- General work abilities.
  Depending on the nature of your job, these can include skills that are often common across jobs. They may include teamwork skills, people skills and customer service.
  These are related to your achievement statements developed earlier.
  - o Work skill area (e.g. communication).
  - o Short sentences or bullet points about your achievements.

It can include other skills and achievements you have already identified. These include word processing, spreadsheets, computer and Internet skills, and software tools.

Identify the work skill area (e.g. word processing).

- o Short sentences or bullet points about your achievements.

- Interests and activities.
  Interests and activities that show your wider interests and abilities. It may include contributory roles to sporting groups or other organisations.

- Referees.
  Two options: list contact names and numbers of your selected referees or "Referees can be supplied on request".

- Contact details.
  Same comments as for resume option one (see above under personal details).

- o Name.

- o Address.

- o Phone.

- o Email.

For an example of this type of resume, see Appendix Resources 6: Foundation Resume example 2 or download the digital version from the book's eResource website.

See the References: eResource link at the end of the chapter.

Follow links to the Appendices: Resources or Templates <TAB> Resumes/CVs <TAB>.

12.6 Personal Plan: Foundation Resume – key points

For your Personal Plan, we will use Resume contents option one outlined above as a possible resume format. The main sections are:

- Career goals.
- Overview of skills and capabilities.

- General skills: draw on your Personal Plan 10: General Achievements for this.
- Other skills and achievements.
- Key qualifications.
- Employment experience.

To download the eResource digital Appendices: Personal Plan, follow the instructions in the References at the end of the chapter.

These concise achievement statements you will create will be expanded later to form part of your Foundation Resume.

Now commence your Personal Plan for Foundation Resume: stage 1.

12.7   Creating your Foundation Resume: stage 1

Creating Your Foundation Resume

The options for your Foundation Resume as previously outlined are:

- use one of the resume examples in this book; or
- use a free resume template from many university websites and career advice centres; or
- use a resume template from a job search agency; or
- use a free resume template from YouExec.

The links for all the above resume templates can be downloaded from the book's eResource website. See the References: eResources link at the end of this chapter.

You have completed Appendix Personal Plan 12: Foundation Resume: stage 1and have key information for your resume.

The steps are:

- Use your selected digital resume template for your Foundation Resume.
- Use the concise achievement statements from your Personal Plan (in this chapter) for input into your resume.

● Transfer or just copy the achievement statements from your Personal Plan to your selected Foundation Resume format.

Whichever resume layout option you select it is not final or fixed. In Chapter 15: Preparing your targeted resume: country-specific, you will be given options to select a resume layout that is appropriate to your target country.

12.8 Summary

In this chapter on Foundation Resume: Stage 1, the initial content for a good resume was introduced. The focus is on the content. It can be arranged later to fit different resume formats or layouts that are used in different countries.

Tips on presentation techniques are important, along with layout and content. The aim is to ensure your resume is visually attractive, easy to read (by the selection panel), and conveys your achievements and abilities.

Examples of resumes have been provided in the Appendices and on the eResources website.

You have selected a resume template. You have converted or copied your achievements from your Personal Plan into your Foundation Resume.

Now you are well on your way to developing a valuable resource for your job search, your Foundation Resume.

The second part of your Foundation Resume: stage 2 is in the next chapter and is related to specific job criteria.

12.9 References and further reading

Innes, J. (2009) *The CV Book: Your Definitive Guide to Writing the Perfect CV.* (Pearson Education Ltd., London, UK).

Rosenberg, A.D. (2008) *The Resume Handbook: How to write Outstanding Resumes and Cover Letters for Every Situation.* (Adams Media, Avon, USA).

YouExec, *Resume Templates and other Career Resources.* www.youexec. com or access via the book's eResource webpage.

Here are several links on options on design or layout of your resume, to suit your own individuality and personality. If you are applying for a job in another country than your own, then check any special resume/CV requirements or format used in that country:

www.canva.com/learn/50-inspiring-resume-designs/

Or via the short cut: https://tinyurl.com/nf8uzcc
www.hongkiat.com/blog/beautiful-resume-design/

Or via the short cut: https://tinyurl.com/qjnes3v
https://creativemarket.com/blog/how-to-design-a-resume

Or via the short cut: https://tinyurl.com/mkfpytf
https://colorlib.com/wp/free-resume-templates/

Or via the short cut: https://tinyurl.com/krwj3ga

12.9.1 Reference: eResource link for this book

For added resources and digital files related to this chapter:

Search: Routledge Text Books or go to: www.routledge.com/

Search window: type "Your Career", which will take you to the eResources for this book.

Or via the short cut: https://tinyurl.com/kyxnfaq

Then go to either:

- Appendices <TAB> Resources <TAB> (Appendices: Resources); or
- Templates <TAB> and the range of resume options; or
- Appendices <TAB> Personal Plan <TAB> (Appendices: Personal Plan); or
- Web References <TAB> References <TAB>.

 **13**

Preparing your Foundation Resume

Stage 2

13.1 Introduction

This chapter will further develop your Foundation Resume. It uses the extended achievement statements you developed in your Personal Plan: Achievements Extended. These were for job-specific criteria: profession, job and personal. In the previous chapter you will have selected a format for your Foundation Resume.

The chapter includes checks to ensure your resume has a positive impact. In Chapter 15 we will assist you to rearrange the Foundation Resume if required. This adaption to a Targeted Resume will allow you to use common layouts for different countries.

13.2 Foundation Resume: stage 2 – contents

Foundation Resume

The purpose of this chapter is to expand your Foundation Resume for a specific job and criteria. The three areas to focus on are professional criteria, job-specific requirements and personal achievements. You will use your Achievements Extended that you have already developed.

13.3   Personal Plan: Foundation Resume – stage 2

The source material you will use is in Appendix Personal Plan 11: Achievements Extended. In the following four sections you will convert these into statements in your Personal Plan: Foundation Resume – stage2. These will cover specific criteria related to the profession, job criteria and personal achievements (directly related to the job).

13.3.1   Profession-specific

Resume: Profession-Specific

For each profession there are profession-specific requirements to meet. For your selected profession, the Achievements Extended statements have already been completed. These were done in your Personal Plan 11: Achievements Extended.

Now complete the Appendix Personal Plan 13: Foundation Resume – stage 2 for profession-specific criteria.

13.3.2   Job-specific

Job-specific skills and achievements are listed in the criteria for a particular job.

Resume: Job-Specific

For a particular job criterion, your Achievements Extended statements have already been completed. These were done in your Personal Plan 11: Achievements Extended.

Now complete the Appendix Personal Plan 13: Foundation Resume – stage 2 for job criteria.

13.3.3   Personal achievements

These may be added skills or achievements from other activities you have done. Perhaps a role in a sporting organisation, volunteer activities, part-time roles or other awards. They should be significant and relate to the job. If none come to mind, then do not worry. It is better to just omit this part than try to concoct something that does not provide a link between yourself and the job.

Resume: Personal Achievements

Any special personal achievements were identified and described in your Personal Plan. These were done in your Personal Plan 11: Achievements Extended.

Now complete the Appendix Personal Plan 13: Foundation Resume – stage 2 for personal aspects.

13.3.4   Referees

You will need to select around three referees to include in your resume. These will be people who will vouch for you if contacted by the organisation that you are applying to. You will need to ask them for permission to include them as a referee for your job application and resume. Outline to them the broad area that you are looking for a job. Send them a copy of your resume as it will help them if they are responding to an enquiry. It avoids sending excessive material (references) to a potential employer (unless this is specifically requested).

Some organisations may prefer written references. This would generally be specified. Usually, it is better to include just the referees' telephone number, email and postal address. The advantage is to keep your application compact. Excessive material such as references can be counterproductive; it can be an extra burden of material for the hiring manager or interview panel to read.

Support Your Application with Referees

For an employer, it is much easier to phone referees once you have reached the interview stage.

Further details on good techniques for obtaining referees and references are covered in Chapter 14: Referees and references. It outlines techniques for requesting and selecting references, options to add them to your application as well as checks and formats for references.

Now complete the Appendix Personal Plan 13: Foundation Resume – stage 2 for referees.

13.4 Creating your Foundation Resume – stage 2

Creating Your Foundation Resume

After you have completed the Personal Plan for this chapter you have key information for your resume.

You will have selected a template for your resume in the previous chapter.

Use the material from your Personal Plan (in this chapter) to create your Foundation Resume. We would recommend you start compiling your resume in a digital format (using the selected resume template). Copy and edit your achievements from your Personal Plan to your Foundation Resume.

This second stage of your resume builds in profession, job criteria and personal aspects into the resume.

13.5 Foundation Resume check

Resume Check

Once you completed your draft Foundation Resume ask someone (preferably with a professional background) to check it. You are asking for their advice on the overall presentation and content. The format and layout can be changed later. This is an option covered later in Chapter 15.

Ask the person doing the check if it comes across as:

- Professional, well presented and succinct?

- Easy to read?

- Presenting key information about you?
- A good reflection of you, your achievements and your potential?
- Easily assessed by a potential manager and interview panel?

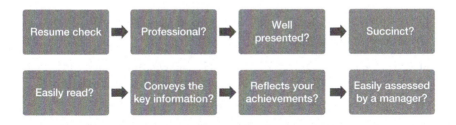

Review the suggestions and make any necessary changes. At this point, this is your Foundation Resume. It is a resource for you. It is a compilation of your abilities, achievements, education and experience. It can be adapted later to fit particular country resume layout format. This adaption is done later in Chapter 15 to create your Targeted Resume.

13.6 Summary

This chapter has extended your Foundation Resume. It has focused mainly on profession- and job-specific aspects as well as personal qualities. The resume you have complied up to this point is a summary of your education, work experience and achievements. It contains key resume aspects you can also add into online bios for social media.

It provides information you will draw on for your final Targeted Resume (Chapter 15). This approach has allowed you to focus on the resume content first and then adapt it later to a particular format for a region.

It is a valuable resource document you should keep. Ensure it is up to date as it is a record of your achievements. It contains much more than is allowed to be included in resumes that are often required to be just one, two or three pages.

This chapter has included a review and check of your resume by some-one else. It is important to fine tune your resume material. In the next chapter we will help you manage your referees: how to request a reference; how to select a referee; and other aspects of referees as added support.

13.7 References and further reading

Barron, D. (2017) *Resume: The Definitive Guide on Writing a Professional Resume to Land You Your Dream Job.* (Create Space, North Charleston, SC, USA).

Ellis, T. (2016) *RIP the Resume: Job Search & Interview Power Prep.* (Peterson's, Albany, USA).

Hanson, C.W. (2017) *Resume Writing 2017: The Ultimate Guide to Writing a Resume that Lands YOU the Job!* (Create Space, North Charleston, SC, USA).

YouExec. *Resume Templates and Other Career Resources.* www.youexec.com

13.7.1 Reference: eResources link for this book

For added resources and digital files related to this chapter:

Search: Routledge Text Books or go to: www.routledge.com/

Search window: type "Your Career", which will take you to the eResources for this book.

Or via the short cut: https://tinyurl.com/kyxnfaq

Then go to either:

- Appendices <TAB> Resources <TAB> (Appendices: Resources); or Appendices <TAB> Personal Plan <TAB> (Appendices: Personal Plan).

Referees and references

14.1 Introduction

References and referees allow potential employers to assess you further. From your perspective (as a job seeker) it is an added way for you to project a positive image (via your references) when seeking a job.

The following chapter is about ways to seek and manage your referees. It will help you answer key questions about referees and references. What are the different ways to arrange references? Who should you ask for references? How to select your referees carefully? How to find out what they are going to say? How to ask for a letter of recommendation? How to ask for LinkedIn recommendations? They draw on advice from experts.

14.2 Referees and references

14.2.1 Ways to arrange references

Contact potential referees who know you and may be prepared to act as referees.

What are some options to handle referees or reference requests? You can ask them to:

- Be a phone referee for possible follow up from a potential employer.

- Provide you with a written reference.

- Provide you with a written reference: you provide a draft outline related to the employment you are seeking.

- Provide a simpler reference via an online social media site (such as LinkedIn).

The pros and cons of these are covered in the following sections.

Ways to Arrange References

It is important that your request is done in the right way. In all of these you need to brief the person about the type of new position you are seeking. That way, they can tailor their reference to the career or job you are seeking, rather than just providing a general reference.

When you are asked to provide a professional reference, this is seeking a recommendation from someone who can vouch for you. It may be your part-time employer, a past employer, or someone who knows you well from a volunteer position or sporting body. It may be someone who is in a professional role and knows you personally and can vouch for your character and values. For new graduates, it may include a university professor or lecturer. Your supervisor of your dissertation or of some assignments you did during your university studies is normally a good choice, as he or she knows not only your work, but also you as a person.

14.2.2   Who to ask for references?

Who should you approach to provide the best reference related to the job you are seeking?

Alison Doyle, a career expert, advises:

> Consider the qualifications for your target job as you are choosing individuals to act as your references. Ask yourself who can vouch for the skills and attributes in your background that are most critical for success in that job.
>
> So your mix of references might differ based on the varied requirements of the positions for which you are applying. The ideal reference will be able to speak in a very specific way about your assets and back up his or her assertions with examples from your work.

Further advice from Doyle includes:

- Ensure the individual you select is comfortable providing a positive recommendation.

- Employers on average check three references for each candidate, so have at least that many ready to vouch for you.

- Know your referees and get their permission to use them.

- You need responsive people that can confirm that you worked there, your reason for leaving and other details.

See Doyle, *Job Search – Professional References*, in the References at the end of this chapter.

Select Your References Carefully

14.2.3 Select your references carefully

Lipschultz, a professional recruiter, on choosing the right reference for the right situation, advises that different references may have different levels of credibility and authority in different industries or professions; therefore, carefully selecting the references for a specific employer may increase the probability of landing that job.

Another reason to limit access to your list of references is that you might want different references depending on the job you have applied for. In most cases, having supervisors (even part-time work, volunteer roles or roles within bodies such as a sporting bodies) carry the most weight. Personal references about your character can also be useful, but not to the same extent as work related ones.

See Lipschultz, *Effective Job Search References*, in the References at the end of this chapter.

14.2.4 How to manage your references

When you get to the stage after an interview where the hiring organisation asks for references, you are close to getting the job. This is an important final step. You want your referees and references to help you to that job offer.

Lipschultz, on effective job search references, advises:

> Sometimes the "reference check" is the tipping point in a hiring manager's decision process. You may be in a virtual tie for the job with someone else, and references may differentiate the two of you.

Bad feedback from a reference could make the company rethink their opinion of you. Obviously, your references are an important part of the process, so you must be very careful how you select and prepare them.

See Lipschultz, *Effective Job Search References*, in the References at the end of this chapter. Make sure your references are available to respond to the hiring organisation's request in a timely fashion. It might be that the persons nominated as your referees are travelling or not available for some time.

14.2.5 How to ask for a letter of recommendation

Alison Doyle advises:

> Don't ask 'Could you write a letter of reference for me?' Just about anyone can write a letter. The problem can be what they are going to write about. Rather, ask: 'Do you feel you know my work well enough to write me a good recommendation letter?' or 'Do you feel you could give me a good reference?' That way, your reference writer has an easy out if they are not comfortable writing a letter and you can be assured that those who say 'yes' will be enthusiastic about your performance and will write a positive letter.

Alternatively:

> When requesting that an individual to act as a reference ask: 'Are you comfortable providing a very positive recommendation for me for (type of job)...I'm trying to make a strong case for my candidacy?' Making your request in writing is usually the best approach so a reluctant individual can decline more comfortably.

You can offer to provide an updated copy of your resume so the reference writer has current information to work with. It is wise to plan ahead and have a list of referees and some letters of recommendation already available. Be prepared when a prospective employer requests references.

How do you find out what they are going to say? Rather than just asking a potential referee to provide their contact details to support your job application, ask them to compose a reference for your file.

See Doyle, *Job Search – Professional References*, in the References at the end of this chapter.

14.2.6   Providing references

When applying for a job, you may be asked for a list of referees either after a job interview or in some cases when you apply for a job. You may choose to add them to your resume. Information to provide includes: the person's name, job title, company, telephone number and email address. Check you have the referees' permission to use them as a reference before you give out their contact information.

It is important to keep referees updated on your progress and let them know if you think they might be contacted. Update them if you have reached the interview stage and let them know any key aspects that you feel may be important for that job. This will help them in making their recommendation for you.

14.2.7   Prepare your referees properly

Lipschultz recommends letting your referees know that they may receive a call regarding a reference. Also, let them know the organisation and the nature of the job. If there are some key aspects related to the job criteria, let them know. This may include unique qualities they are seeking.

See Lipschultz, *Effective Job Search References*, in the References at the end of this chapter.

14.2.8   LinkedIn references

LinkedIn allows you to have references and referees linked to your profile. This means potential employers can directly approach your referees without your approval. It can mean that the referee process is out of your hands. You are unable to remind referees about upcoming jobs and the organisation that may contact them.

14.2.8.1 How to ask for a LinkedIn reference

The LinkedIn Help centre provides advice on how to request a recommendation:

- LinkedIn has the advantage and ability to request recommendations from contacts, affiliates, current and former supervisors, etc.

- These recommendations serve as references for potential employers. A profile with several positive recommendations from other professionals carries added weight for those interviewing and selecting applicants.

- Writing a recommendation takes time. A positive suggestion is for you to "write a draft version" for them first. Be honest and realistic. Request recommendations from previous supervisors and co-workers. It will add to your profile.

How to Ask for a LinkedIn Reference

On LinkedIn, you can ask your connections to write a recommendation of your work that you can display on your profile:

- Move your cursor over your photo in the top right of your homepage and select **Privacy & Settings.** You may be prompted to **Sign in.**

- Under the Helpful Links section, select **Manage your recommendations**.

- Click the **Ask for recommendations** tab at the top of the page.

- Follow the prompts to request the recommendation.

- Click **Send.**

Note: You can request a recommendation from up to 3 connections at once. There's no limit to the total number of recommendations you can request or receive.

See LinkedIn Help Centre: Request a Recommendation, in the References at the end of this chapter.

Make it Easy for Referees

Joshua Waldman at Career Realism advises on how to ask for a new reference without burdening your manager or mentor:

- Remind them that a LinkedIn recommendation isn't a full letter; it takes only about 10 minutes and doesn't need to be longer than three short paragraphs.

- Give them something specific to recommend about you. For example, "Would you mind talking about the (project) we did together and the role I played?"

- Suggest three specific personality or professional traits you want them to mention. For example, "Would you mind mentioning my work ethic, ability to work in teams, and depth of experience working with large enterprise accounts?"

See Waldman, *LinkedIn Recommendations*, in the References at the end of this chapter.

14.3 Personal Plan: Foundation Resume – referees

From the advice above and for the selected job you should have selected several referees to add to your Personal Plan.

Now complete Appendix Personal Plan 13: Foundation Resume – stage 2 for referees.

14.4 Creating your Foundation Resume: referees

Creating Your Foundation Resume

From the Personal Plan completed above, you identified and added the details of selected referees. These are relevant for this particular job and can support your application. For other types of jobs, you may choose other referees.

Convert or copy your referee details from your Personal Plan to your Foundation Resume. This will complete your comprehensive Foundation Resume document – a resource of your abilities, experience and achievements. It is a document that you will draw on for job applications. It is much larger than a typical job resume (which is usually one to two pages), but contains added information that is valuable for interviews and different job applications as well.

14.5 Summary

In summary, this chapter on referees and references is a key part of securing a job. It is about how you approach potential referees and about keeping them informed so that they can represent you in ways that relate to the job you are applying for.

The preceding advice from experts will help you decide who to approach for a reference, how to ask for a letter of recommendation and preparing your referees properly.

Options on how to use LinkedIn to manage your reference requests were outlined.

Social media is making it easier for you to request a reference online. It is also making it easier for referees to compile a short recommendation for you online.

References play a key role in your job search process.

You have converted or copied the material from your Personal Plan into your Foundation Resume.

In the next chapter, we will provide an overview of different resume formats for different countries. You will be then able to modify the layout (and order of contents) of your Foundation Resume into a Targeted Resume that is country-specific.

We have adopted this approach so the focus has been on the content material of your resume.

The Foundation Resume is a key resource.

14.6 References and further reading

Bodine, P. (2010) *Perfect Phrases for Letters of Recommendation*. (McGraw-Hill, New York, NY, USA). Doyle, A. (2017) *Job Search – Professional References.* http://jobsearch.about.com/od/professionalreferences/f/professional-references.htm

Fawcett, S.R. (2014) *Instant Recommendation Letter Kit: How to Write Winning Letters of Recommendation*. (McGraw-Hill, New York, NY, USA, 4th edn).

LinkedIn Help Centre. Request a Recommendation. www.linkedin.com/help/linkedin?lang=en

Lipschultz, J. *Effective Job Search References*. Job Hunt. www.job-hunt.org/recruiters/effective-job-search-references.shtml or via the short cut: https://tinyurl.com/kqjyjvb

Waldman, J. (2013) *How to Ask for LinkedIn Recommendations*. Career Realism. www.careerealism.com/linkedin-recommendations/ or via the short cut: https://tinyurl.com/m5kc3o9

Whalley, S. (2000) *How to Write Powerful Letters of Recommendation*. (Educational Media, Warminster, PA, USA).

14.6.1 Reference: eResources link for this book

For added resources and digital files related to this chapter:

Search: Routledge Text Books or go to: www.routledge.com/

Search window: type "Your Career", which will take you to the eResources for this book.

Or via the short cut: https://tinyurl.com/kyxnfaq

Then go to:

- Appendices <TAB> Personal Plan <TAB> (Appendices: Personal Plan).

Preparing your Targeted Resume

Country-specific

15.1 Introduction

The first part of this chapter will address some of the broader differences in formats for different countries or regions. We will then address some of the main differences for a selection of countries or regions. We have selected Australia and New Zealand, UK, USA, Europe, Asia, Canada, South America and China. We suggest you scan through the relevant section for your region. The overall message is that there is no one size fits all for a resume layout, even within a country.

There are a very large range of options and variations in resume layouts or formats. From an international perspective or even a country perspective, we cannot definitively cover all variations. We seek to alert you to some of the types of differences you may encounter and encourage you to adapt to the country format relevant to your job application. The chapter reflects on the multitude of variations and an option on how to address this.

In the preceding chapters, we have helped you compile your achievements and experience into a Foundation Resume; the focus is on helping you create the resume content. This chapter is the next stage. The reader can research local preferred formats, contextual and cultural variations. The web is the best resource to reflect these variations. You will choose your final resume layout.

Aim – Targeted Resume

We suggest you scan the section related to your target country or region, before going to the action section near the end to create your Targeted Resume using the Personal Plan for guidance. You will adapt your

Foundation Resume to the country format that is applicable to the job you are seeking. This becomes your Targeted Resume, which is the outcome of this chapter.

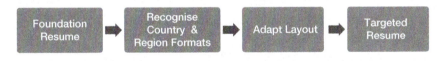

15.2 Country and regional variations for resumes

Resume Variations: Countries and Regions

There are differences in resume formats between countries and even within countries. This chapter provides an overview of the differences to help you select the most appropriate format. Because of the differences, it is up to the reader to check local resume formats and common layouts. It is generally advisable to use a locally accepted format. You want your resume to be broadly similar to others that will be submitted. You are trying to avoid submitting a resume that may be fine for one country, but inappropriate for another country that uses a different format.

We have sought to provide an overview in the sections below of some resume characteristics for:

- Australia and New Zealand.
- United Kingdom (UK).
- United States of America (USA).
- Europe.
- Asia.
- Canada.
- South America.
- China.

These are broad reviews. Some indicative examples are contained in the Appendix Resources 10 to 14: Targeted Resume – country.

To help you select a resume template the following options are available:

- resume examples in this book;
- free resume template from many university websites and career advice centres;
- resume template from a job search agency; and
- free resume template from YouExec.

These can be downloaded from the eResources. To access the eResources go to the References: eResources link at end of this chapter.

More examples can be found via websites and the references found at the end of this chapter. The web is the best resource for different resume formats for a multiplicity of countries. The reader is best placed to research the optimum resume format for their country and career area via the web.

The information you have complied can easily be edited into the selected format.

15.3 Australia and New Zealand: resume formats

Australia and New Zealand: Resumes

This section aims to give you a feel for different formats and resume layout options that are commonly used in Australia and New Zealand. Please note there are many variations that are used. We will try and focus on the main layout structure and common contents.

It is up to the reader to check these options and select a final layout that is appropriate.

15.3.1 Australia and New Zealand: resume tips

The broad sections for Australia and New Zealand resumes include:

- Contact details.
- Career objective.

- Education and training.

- Employment history.

- Skills and competencies: summary.

- Extra-curricular activities and interests.

- Memberships.

- Referees.

Some formats may also include:

- Practicums and industrial experience.

- Conferences or papers presented.

- Residency, visa or work permit.

The most common format for employment history is reverse chronological (latest employment comes first); added information includes: position title; organisation; dates (months/year); and responsibilities.

- Resume order: You can choose to change the order of the content in your resume. The aim is to ensure it is tailored to the job, its specifications and the employer's requirements. It should be concise and highlight the key information you want to convey including your appropriateness for the position.

- Personal contact details: The main details required are name, address, telephone numbers and email.

- Achievements and awards: Highlight any significant achievements. This could include awards, prizes or high grades. These highlight added effort and performance.

- Career objective: It is a short statement that highlights what you are aiming for in the prospective job. It can reflect your motivation and enthusiasm for the job.

- Extra-curricular activities and interests: It will let the employer get a wider view of you and you interests. Even activities not directly related to the job can show characteristics such as commitment, energy, diverse skills and other personal attributes.

- Membership: Including associate membership of a professional organisation can show an added commitment to the profession. It can also reflect an interest in ongoing professional growth.

- Photograph: It is not usually recommended or encouraged. The important part of your resume is the content, not your appearance.

15.3.2 Australia and New Zealand: resume examples – website links

Some university websites with resume formats and advice include: Sydney University, Resume contents and examples.

https://sydney.edu.au/careers/students/applying-for-jobs/how-to-write-a-resume.html or via the short cut: https://tinyurl.com/ybkthqez

University of New South Wales, Resume tips, contents and examples. https://student.unsw.edu.au/resume-tips-answers

Graduate Careers Australia (GCA), www.graduatecareers.com.au/careerplanningandresources/preparingyourapplication/allaboutapplications/

Queensland University of Technology (QUT), Resume resources and examples of resumes for different faculties/ professions. www.careers.qut.edu.au/student/resume.jsp

Griffith University, Queensland, Resume examples. www.griffith.edu.au/careers-employment/get-job-ready/resumes

CareersNZ is a government agency that provides assistance with job hunting. Their website contains useful resources and resume examples: www.careers.govt.nz/job-hunting/cvs-and-cover-letters/templates/#cID_500

15.3.3 Australia and New Zealand: resume format

Examples of resume formats are in:

- Appendix Resources 5: Foundation Resume example 1.
- Appendix Resources 6: Foundation Resume example 2.
- Appendix Resources 10: Targeted Resume – Australian example.

There is no one standard layout. These are indicative examples.

Other resume templates are available from the eResources. See the link at the end of this chapter.

Alternatively, another major resource for resume formats is the web.

To guide you through these steps, use your Personal Plan. Jump to the end of this chapter.

Go to section 15.11: Creating your Targeted Resume (country-specific).

15.4 UK: resume formats

United Kingdom: Resumes

This section aims to give you a feel for some UK resume characteristics.

Please note there are many variations that are used. We will try and focus on the main layout structure and common contents. It is up to the reader to check these options and select a final layout that is appropriate.

15.4.1 UK: resume tips

- Resume order: You can choose to change the order of the content in your resume. The aim is to ensure it is tailored to the job, its specifications and employers' requirements. It should be concise and highlight the key information you want to convey including your appropriateness for the position. Follow the layout structure that is common for your region.

- Spelling: Use a spelling and grammar checker that uses UK English.

- Photograph: Do not include a photo. Many specialists advise against this. It tends to change the focus in your application from your skills and qualifications to the less significant aspect of appearance.

- Layout: Variations exists between organisations. Some adopt a layout like this:

  o Name and contact details.

  o Personal statement.

  o Education: tertiary.

    ▪ University degree and years attended.

    ▪ Major units or modules.

    ▪ High achievements.

- o Education: high school:
  - School and years attended.
  - Final results.
- o Work experience and employment (most recent first):
  - Company (dates: from; to).
  - Position.
  - Roles and skills acquired.
- o Areas of expertise and professional skills:
  - Key skills or achievements.
  - Profession-specific.
  - Job-specific.
- o Personal skills (paragraph to highlight your personal attributes that relate to the job).
- o Interests and achievements (paragraph to highlight your personal attributes that relate to the job).
- o References.

See CV-Library UK, in the References at the end of this chapter.
Modelo Curriculum advises:

> Format and layout:
> Keep it to two pages. The reasons for applying are in the cover letter not the resume.
> References:
> Recommendations are important in UK hiring processes. A majority of employers get in touch with referees. Include at least two referees.
> Include: name, position, address and phone number.
> Many organisations suggest: "Referees available on request" instead of listing the references.
> The option of providing the referees is possibly more helpful for the employing organisation.
> Personal Achievements: Include personal achievements, leadership roles and hobbies.

Focus: ensure the focus is on candidate's skills and experience.
American format: Modelo Curriculum advises:

> Many British enterprises prefer a CV with an
> American format, which starts with the most
> recent job. This kind of CV is less structured and
> sometimes shorter than the typical one. How-
> ever, it can also consist of 3 to 5 pages . . . the
> professional goal is included. Work experience
> is listed with latest position first.

See Modelo Curriculum in the References at the end of this chapter.

15.4.2 UK: resume examples – website links

Some university websites with resume formats and advice include:
University of Kent, Example CVs. www.kent.ac.uk/careers/cv/cvexamples.
  htm

University of Manchester, Example CVs. www.careers.manchester.ac.uk/
  applicationsinterviews/cv/examplecvs/

University of Oxford, Careers and CVs. www.careers.ox.ac.uk/cvs/

15.4.3 UK: resume format

An example of a UK resume format is given in the Appendix Resources 11:
Targeted Resume – UK example.

There is no one standard layout. This is an indicative example.

Other resume templates are available from the eResources. See the
link at the end of this chapter. Alternatively, another major resource for
resume formats is the web. To guide you through these steps, use your
Personal Plan. Jump to the end of this chapter at section 15.11: Creating
your Targeted Resume (country-specific).

15.5 USA: resume formats

USA: Resumes

This section aims to give you a feel for some USA resume characteristics.

Please note there are many variations that are used. We will try and focus on the main layout structure and common contents. It is up to the reader to check these options and select a final layout that is appropriate.

15.5.1 USA: main resume types

- Chronological: work experience in chronological order (usually reverse order with latest first).
- Functional: focuses on acquired skills and is often good for new graduates.
- Combined or hybrid: combines chronological and functional.
- Federal: USAJOBS – USA government website and format for resumes for federal government jobs.
- Curriculum Vitae (CV): more extensive and primarily used in academia, scientific research and academic teaching roles.

See American University, in the References at the end of this chapter.

Explore these options via web links to help decide the resume type and layout format you wish to use. You may want to look at different resume types and examples to help choose.

Job search websites can contain advice on resumes, templates or resume builder tools. They contain examples for different career areas. The challenge can be too much information.

See Live Career, in the References at the end of this chapter.

- Basic resume sections. These are common to main resume types:
  - Contact information.
  - Resume summary or objective.
  - Education.
  - Experience or work history.
  - Skills.
- Objective: Concise statement on your career goal and why you are seeking the position.
- Education:
  - Educational institution and its location by city and state.
  - Most recent degree you are pursuing or have gained; list additional degrees in reverse chronological order.

- o Degree level; major, minor or concentration; and the month and year of graduation or anticipated completion.
- o Scholarships, academic awards can be included under education or outlined separately.
- o Relevant courses and major projects relevant to the position and career area.
- Experience or work history:
  - o Emphasise relevant work experience.
  - o Can include: paid full-time work, part time, internships, volunteer roles and leadership roles.
  - o Organisation and its location by city and state, position title and employment dates (month and year).
  - o Use concise statements.
  - o Describe your knowledge and skills acquired.
- Skills: American University, Washington suggests sub categories for skills:
  - o Language skills.
  - o Computer skills.
  - o Special skills such analysis, training and public speaking.
  - o Leadership or community activities: information on skills that could benefit the position you are seeking. It could be leadership roles, activities or sports.
  - o These can show evidence of teamwork, communication and other valuable skills.
- Training: Certificates gained.
- Activities: Extra-curricular activities and accomplishments so employers can see your broader interests and abilities.
- Professional associations: List organisations you have been a member of that relate to the career.

See American University, in the References at the end of this chapter.

15.5.2 USA: federal resume

- Same content as a resume.

- Added information required for federal applications (such as your social security number, country of citizenship, position details, high school credentials, salary history and references).

- Employment history.

- Education.

- Training and skills (reverse chronological order).

- You need an account with USAJOBS to access the resume builder.

- To create one uniform resume that includes all of the information required by government agencies, use the USAJOBS Resume Builder.

See the USAJOBS website in the References at the end of this chapter.

See also the USAJOBS Resume Builder in the References at the end of this chapter.

USAJOBS automatically provides a list of available resumes and documents to attach to your application. It only allows documents the hiring agency is willing to accept.

15.5.3 USA: resume tips

- Size: one to two pages.

- Contact: include email.

- Check for spelling errors and grammar.

- Do not include a photo.

- Do not include gender and religion.

- Include GPA (grade point average) under education.

- Employment: concisely describe what you achieved in two to three sentences.

- Put your most recent work first (reverse chronological).

- Use a US grammar and spell checker.

Berkeley University of California, Career Center advises that a USA resume includes:

- One page.
- Personal contact information.
- Links to websites or LinkedIn profile (optional).
- Education (degrees).
- Relevant course work (optional).
- Relevant experiences such as:
  - Research experiences.
  - Course and independent projects.
  - Student leadership.
  - Volunteering.
  - Skills (language, computer, etc.).

Support: they recommend advice from a career counsellor and support from friends. Universities have career counselling services.

USA resumes usually do not include:

- Personal information such as: age, gender, marital status, race or ethnicity, home country.
- Immigration status.
- Photograph.
- Religion.
- International permanent address.

See Berkeley University of California, Career Center in the References at the end of this chapter.

CareerOne® is a career and employment company. It advises that common resume blunders are:

- Spelling mistakes.
- Unattractive format and layout.

- Confessing to hobbies like drinking with mates.
- Including useless information.
- Too long.

See Career One, *Resume and Cover Letter*, in the References at the end of this chapter.

The purpose of your resume is to get an interview. Your resume must be strong and attract interest.

It is clear that there are a number of layout options for your resume. Select a layout that is widely used and accepted. In essence, the content is very similar. Remember only a small amount of time is spent reviewing a resume. This does not mean it is unimportant; quite the opposite in fact. It is a crucial entry to a job interview. Your effort spent getting the contents (and layout right) are great investments.

15.5.4 USA: resume format

An example of a US resume format is given in Appendix Resources 12: Targeted Resume – USA example.

There is no one standard layout. This is an indicative example.

Other resume templates are available from the eResources. See the link at the end of this chapter. Alternatively, another major resource for resume formats is the web. To guide you through these steps, use your Personal Plan. Jump to the end of this chapter. Go to section 15.11: Creating your Targeted Resume (country-specific).

15.6 Europe: resume formats

Europe: Resumes

This section will give you a feel for some European resume (or CV) characteristics. Please note there are many variations that are used. As well as variation within the 28 member countries of the European Union, there are other European countries that are not part of the EU that have resume variations. Curriculum vitae (CV) is widely used; we will mainly use the generic term resume apart from specific CV labelled documents.

Significantly, there has been a major initiative to introduce a common EU Europass CV. We will outline its characteristics and useful links. In some countries and organisations, the US format is used at times. No one size fits all. We will try and focus on the common contents. It is up to the reader to select a final layout that is appropriate. The Foundation Resume you have created is a valuable resource if you choose to complete online templates such as the Europass CV.

15.6.1 *Europe: resume variations*

There are significant variations in the contents as well as common information between European countries. The following is intended to reflect some of the differences. It is not intended to be comprehensive for a particular country. The aim is to give some examples to alert the reader to check for country and regional differences in both resumes and cover letters.

The principle we have followed throughout is that the content of your Foundation Resume is most important initially. The reformatting to a different country requirement in your Targeted Resume is a final editing stage.

The following should be quickly scanned; it is intended to reflect the range of differences that exist more than details. Its purpose is to show the reader the range of variations.

15.6.1.1 Resume size: select examples

- Belgium: no longer than three pages is advised.
- Spain and Portugal: two to three pages is common.
- Germany: one to two pages.
- The Netherlands: usually one page of facts and cover letter; US resume option is increasing and this is three to five pages with a focus on skills and experience.
- Italy: two pages.
- France: one to three pages.
- Austria: one to three pages, but usually two.

15.6.1.2 Layout order (dates): select examples

- Some countries prefer experience listed in chronological order, earliest first (e.g. Germany and Italy in chronological order); others use reverse chronology with latest employment first.

15.6.1.3 Career goals: select examples

- Included in France.
- Italy: included in cover letter.

15.6.1.4 Personal information: select examples

- Some countries require nationality and marital status (e.g. Belgium); date and place of birth as well as marital status (Spain and Portugal).
- Scandinavia: personal information such as gender, photo or age is not included.
- Germany: personal information such as age, gender, marital status, children, schooling and residency history is included.
- Finland: birth date and birth place are included.
- France: marital status and nationality are included.

15.6.1.5 Education: select examples

- In Belgium, this includes beginning and graduation dates and studies even if you did not complete the programme.
- In Spain and Portugal, list high school including location and graduation date.
- In France, only high school and university diplomas are included.
- In the Netherlands, subjects but not grades.
- In Ireland, include grades for subjects.

15.6.1.6 Student practice: select examples

- Included in Germany.
- Included in France.

15.6.1.7 Professional experience: select examples

- For some countries, include for company information the scope of company activities.
- Include main tasks for every position (e.g. Finland).
- In other countries, the position or role is sufficient.
- The Netherlands: give exact dates.
- France: refer to position, level, responsibilities and dates.

15.6.1.8 Special skills: select examples

- Include computer skills (e.g. Spain and Portugal).

15.6.1.9 Languages: select examples

- Include foreign languages in most resumes (e.g. Germany and France are two examples).
- Belgium: level of knowledge and fluency.
- Include language skills and proficiency (e.g. Spain and Portugal).

15.6.1.10 Military experience: select examples

- Germany: include military and social service details.
- Belgium: include dates of service, where you were based and duties.

15.6.1.11 Personal interests and hobbies: select examples

- Include briefly for Spain and Portugal.
- The Netherlands: include.

- Ireland: include.
- Belgium: include.
- Italy: exclude.
- Denmark: other hobbies, sports and travel are included.

15.6.1.12 Photos: select examples

- Included in some countries, but not in others (e.g. in Denmark they are not necessary). It is common in many European countries, but check differences. They are not included generally in Italy for example, but they are included in Austria. They are recommended for use in many European countries.

15.6.1.13 Other: select examples

- Signing the resume is common in Austria and Germany. In some cases, employers want a handwritten resume.

15.6.1.14 Summary

From the select examples above, it is clear that there are many differences between countries for resumes. The key message is that this is a reformatting and editing phase of your Foundation Resume into your Targeted Resume format. Both are key documents that your retain and can build on. The Foundation Resume can be regarded as a record of your achievements, experience and education. You select from it the parts you need for the particular job application; you also refer to it as you prepare for the interview stage.

The next section introduces the European Union approach to resume standardisation.

See Modelo Curriculum, Resume 2017 and Redstar Resume Publications© in the References at the end of this chapter.

15.6.2 Europass CV

The Europass CV has sought to introduce a common approach across multiple countries that are part of the European Union (EU). It has flexibility in the content layout that can reflect variations and different requirements between countries. It aims to help job seekers communicate skills and qualifications and to help employers understand the workforce's skills and qualifications.

It offers a standard framework for qualifications and competences, plus standardised application documents for different countries.

15.6.2.1   Background

In 2012, the Europass website was extended. It included a new CV (resume) template plus an online editor for CV creation. It added in a European skills passport (ESP) that allowed people to build a folder – an inventory of skills, experience and qualifications. Improved tutorials were included. It can include a language passport, copies of degrees, attestations of employment, etc. When attached to the Europass CV, it brings evidence of skills and qualifications.

See Europass in the References at the end of this chapter.

15.6.2.2   What makes up the Europass?

The main aspects of the Europass are a portfolio of documents:

- Europass CV is a standardised European format for resumes (CVs).
- The Europass Language Passport details the languages and levels of fluency you possess.

In addition, there are documents issued by education and training authorities:

- Europass Mobility Document: records information about your work experience in other countries of the EU.
- Europass Diploma Supplement: records your academic qualifications.
- Europass Certificate Supplement: records your vocational qualifications.

Using the Europass framework aims to help different application documents conform to an agreed format. It seeks to avoid significant changes in job application resumes and qualification documents to adapt to the cultural differences that exist between many European countries.

The Europass CV is the backbone of the Europass portfolio of documents. It provides an online wizard and templates to ensure consistency of headings. You choose which fields to fill in. You can remove any field you like, so that no blank fields appear on the completed Europass CV.

The main fields include:

- Personal details, language proficiency, work experience and educational and training attainments.
- Additional competences, emphasising technical, organisational, artistic and social skills.
- Optional information that might be added to the Europass CV in the form of annexes.

Full details are available on the Europass website (see the References at the end of this chapter). The templates are available in multiple EU languages (seethe Europass templates and Europass CV examples in the References at the end if this chapter).

The Europass CV (or resume) can be completed:

- Online: go to the Europass online editor to complete your CV. You can then download the file or send it to your email account. You will then be able to upload the file to the online editor for updating.
- Offline: download the Europass CV template, instructions and examples. You can then use this information to generate your CV on your computer.

See Europass in the References at the end of this chapter.

The main headings and contents of the Europass CV include the opportunity to fill in details such as:

- Personal information.
- Type of application.
- Work experience.
- Education and training.
- Personal skills:
  - Mother tongue(s).
  - Other language(s).
  - Communication skills.

o Organisational and managerial skills.

o Job-related skills.

o Digital competence.

15.6.3 Europe: resume format

The previous sections have shown the variations that exist within Europe. It is clear that the final format for your application and country can only be selected by the reader.

Several options are available, including:

- Select a resume format that is common for your target country and region.
- Adopt the Europass CV system.
- Use a resume (CV) layout that is based on the Europass format.
- eResources website: This contains other resume templates in download-able Word format.

An example of a European resume format is given in Appendix Resources 13: Targeted Resume – European example. The example is available on the book's eResources website. There is no one standard layout. This is an indicative example. Other resume templates are available from the eResources. See the link at the end of this chapter. To guide you through these steps, use your Personal Plan. Jump to the end of this chapter. Go to section 15.11: Creating your Targeted Resume (country-specific).

15.7 Asia: resume formats

Asia: Resumes

Asia comprises over half the world's population. A region as large as Asia covers major and populous countries such as India and China. We will look at Chinese resumes in section 15.10: China: resume formats, later in this chapter.

It is obvious that there is no one size fits all for resumes. The diversity of cultures is a reflection of the diversity of resume formats. Additionally, most countries in Asia do not use the roman alphabet (except for some of the former English colonial countries). Mongolia, Korea, Japan, China, Thailand, Central Asian countries, Iran, the Arabic countries and several others, all have their own scripts, which should be used in those countries.

It is up to the reader to check these options and select a final layout that is appropriate.

15.7.1 *Asia: resume variations*

There are significant variations in the contents as well as common information between Asian countries. It is not possible nor the aim of the book to reflect all the variations as these are better explored via the web. The following is intended to reflect some of the differences. It is not intended to be comprehensive for a particular country. The aim is to give some examples to alert the reader to check for country and regional differences.

15.7.1.1 Resume size: select examples

- Thailand: two to three pages.
- Singapore: two pages is considered ideal for graduates.

15.7.1.2 Variations:

- Hong Kong: it has a Westernised approach to resumes.
- Japan: check out the standard resume template, Rirekisho. It is not flexible. It is handwritten and includes a photo.
- Singapore: nominating your expected salary. Indicate if it is negotiable.
- India: declaration that the information provided is true.

15.7.1.3 Personal information: Asia

- Resumes contain personal information such as a photograph, gender, marital status, children (some countries), date of birth and nationality, etc.
- Photos are commonly included on resumes.

15.7.1.4   Summary

From the select examples above it is clear that there are many differences between Asian countries for resumes.

Please refer to the following websites in the References at the end of this chapter:

Resume Edge, www.resumeedge.com/resumes-from-around-the-world/

Ashcroft, B. (2013) *Write the Perfect CV for your New Job in Asia*. Expat Job Market, 22.

February.   https://expatjobmarket.com/career-advice/write-the-perfect-cv-asia/

Nanyang Technical University, Singapore, http://ntu.jobscentral.com.sg/files/sample/

JobERA, http://jobera.com/japan/japan-resume-rirekisho.html

City University of Hong Kong, Career and Leadership Centre, www6.cityu.edu.hk/caio/city-u/index.asp and www6.cityu.edu.hk/caio/city-u/page.asp?id=13

15.7.2   Asia: resume format

An example of an Asian resume format is in Appendix Resources 14: Targeted Resume – Asian example. There is no one standard layout. This is an indicative example. Other resume templates are available from the eResources. See the link at the end of this chapter. Alternatively, another major resource for resume formats is the web. To guide you through these steps, use your Personal Plan. Jump to the end of this chapter. Go to section 15.11: Creating your Targeted Resume (country-specific).

15.8   Canada: resume formats

Canada is a bilingual country. Your resume will be in English or French depending on the position. For federal positions, the resume should be in both languages.

Please note there are many variations that are used. We will try and focus on the main layout structure and common contents. It is up to the reader to check these options and select a final layout that is appropriate.

Canada: Resumes

15.8.1 Canada: resume variations

Most resumes are either functional, which is skills–oriented or chronological, which is time- and work experience-based. For new graduates, a functional resume is often a good format.

Canadian resumes are one to two pages long. It is recommended that you use keywords in your resume to describe your skills and qualifications. Often these are keywords used in the description of the position and role.

Personal information such as gender, date of birth or marital status is not entered. Include your mobile phone number and email address. It is recommended that you include a link to your LinkedIn profile also.

15.8.1.1 One or two page typical layout

- Name and contact.
- Education: university degree, years.
- Skills or highlights.
- Languages.
- Work experience.
- Community and volunteer roles.
- Extra-curricular activities.
- Interests.

See McGill University, Montreal: Career Planning Service and Moving 2 Canada: Resume format in Canada, in the References at the end of this chapter.

15.8.2 Canada: resume format

An example of a US resume format is given in Appendix Resources 12: Targeted Resume – USA example. There is no one standard layout. This is an indicative example. Other resume templates are available from the eResources. See the link at the end of this chapter. Alternatively, another major resource for resume formats is the web. To guide you through these steps, use your Personal Plan. Jump to the end of this chapter. Go to section 15.11: Creating your Targeted Resume (country-specific).

15.9   South America: resume formats

South America encompasses Argentina, Bolivia, Brazil, Chile, Colombia, Ecuador, Venezuela, and many more countries besides. The principal language is Spanish except for Brazil, which uses Portuguese. It is obvious that there is no one size fits all for resumes. The diversity of cultures is a reflection of the diversity of resume formats.

South America: Resumes

This section aims to give you a feel for some resume characteristics.

Please note there are many variations that are used. We will try and focus on the main layout structure and common contents. It is up to the reader to check these options and select a final layout that is appropriate

15.9.1   *South America: resume variations*

There are significant variations in the contents as well as information that is common in resumes; these are better explored via the web. The following is intended to reflect some of the differences. It is not intended to be comprehensive for a particular country. The aim is to give some examples to alert the reader to check for country and regional differences.

15.9.1.1   Resume size: select examples

- Many recommend one page.
- Argentina: up to two or three pages.

15.9.1.2   Variations

- For some countries, it is appropriate to include marital status.
- Some use the USA format.
- Others the Spanish format.
- Argentina: cover letter to highlight characteristics that set you apart.

Resumes (CVs) are concise and are usually two or three pages.

It contains contact information, educational background, job history and additional information, such as languages spoken, IT skills, personal interests and specialised courses.

- Brazil: brief cover letter to introduce you and lead the reader to your resume.

  Resumes are concise and are usually two pages and reflect positions held, responsibilities involved, results achieved and other relevant details.

- Chile: brief letter to highlight your achievements. Formal style. Resume should be one page generally. It highlights your skills and achievements relevant to the position.

- Peru: cover letter not usual in most cases. If using one, make it brief and reflect how you stand out. Your resume should emphasise your skills in relation to the position.

15.9.1.3 Personal information: South America

Recommendations include:

- Resumes contain personal information such as gender, nationality and language skills.
- Gender, marital status, children (some countries), date of birth and nationality, etc. can also be included.
- Photos are commonly included on resumes.

15.9.1.4 Photos

South American resumes usually include a photo.

15.9.1.5 Summary

From the select examples above it is clear that there are many differences between South American countries for resumes.

See Going Global and 'What to include in a CV – an international guide', in the References at the end of this chapter.

15.9.2 South America: resume format

There is no one standard layout. Resume templates are available from the eResources. See the link at the end of this chapter. Alternatively, another major resource for resume formats is the web.

To guide you through these steps, use your Personal Plan. Jump to the end of this chapter.

Go to section 15.11: Creating your Targeted Resume (country-specific).

15.10 China: resume formats

China is part of Asia but it warrants a separate section. There are around 7 million graduates each year in China, so job hunting for new graduates is significant. Additionally, China now offers thousands of post-graduate scholarships to foreigners for doing a master's degree or doctorate at a Chinese university. In these cases, your academic resume should be in English, commonly using the US format.

If applying for a job, the resume will predominantly be in Chinese or for some companies in both Chinese and English.

Please note there are many variations that are used. We will try and focus on the main layout structure and common contents. It is up to the reader to check these options and select a final layout that is appropriate.

China: Resumes

15.10.1 China: resume variations

Chinese resumes are similar to resumes elsewhere in the world. They are typically one to two pages long. There are no strict rules. If you are required to submit in both English and Chinese, the total length will be four pages maximum.

Personal information such as gender, date of birth or marital status is included. Include your mobile phone number and email address. A photo is included. It is recommended to include a link to your LinkedIn profile or XING social networking address. Other local social media sites may be more relevant such as "qq" and "WeChat" (the Chinese version of "WhatsApp").

Social networking sites are used by hiring managers to check your application. Ensure it reflects a professional approach. Be humble and polite in your application correspondence. Use keywords that relate to the keywords of the job criteria.

Regarding references, the usual approach is to say "References available on request".

Applying for jobs via the Internet is common in China. Your application will include a cover letter and your resume.

15.10.1.1   One or two page typical layout

- Name and contact details.

- Career objective.

- Education: university degree and years (in reverse chronology, latest first).

- Work experience: in reverse chronology, latest first.

- Skills or other relevant information:

  o Language skills.

  o Computer skills.

  o Professional associations.

  o Extra-curricular activities or interests.

  o References: available on request.

See the following websites in the References at the end of this chapter: JobERA.com, China Resume. http://jobera.com/china/china-resume.html

Hanbridge Mandarin, How to Write a Chinese Resume. www.hanbridgemandarin.com/article/business-chinese-learning-tips/how-to-write-a-chinese-resume/

University of Exeter, Careers and Employment. www.exeter.ac.uk/media/universityofexeter/careersandemployability/globalemployability/pdfs/Chinese_CVs_and_Covering_letter_advice.pdf

See also: Theobald, O. (2016) in the References at the end of this chapter.

15.10.2   China: resume format

There is no one standard layout. Resume templates are available from the eResources. See the link at the end of this chapter. Alternatively another major resource for resume formats is the web. Use the web to identify a resume format that is appropriate for your region (and best reflects the skills of a new graduate).

To guide you through these steps, use your Personal Plan. Jump to the end of this chapter. Go to section 15.11: Creating your Targeted Resume (country-specific).

15.11 Creating your Targeted Resume (country-specific)

The final stage of your resume process is to reformat your Foundation Resume into the format you have selected for your target country.

Create Your Targeted Resume

In earlier chapters you selected a resume format for your Foundation Resume. It does not have to be the format you use for your final resume and job application. Options available for your Targeted Resume template include:

- The eResources for this book. Resume examples are available via the eResources website for this book and are in downloadable digital Word format.

  Go to the References: eResources link at the end of this chapter.

  In the eResources: follow the links to the Templates <TAB> and resume options.

  These include Resumes/CV <TAB> and Free Resume <TAB>.

  Select your preferred template then download it and save to your PC.

- Free resume templates from many university websites and career advice centres.
- Resume templates from a job search agency (either free or combined with paid job search service).

The aim is to select a resume format relevant for graduates, your profession and in a format that is accepted for your country or region.

Select a suitable resume layout for your country or region. Follow the advice and options above including the eResources website digital material.

15.12   Personal Plan: Targeted Resume

See Appendix Personal Plan 14: Targeted Resume (country format). This will guide you through the main steps to create your Targeted Resume.

In essence, you will select and transfer information from your Foundation Resume to your Targeted Resume format. It will be a compact version of one to two pages that is appropriate to the formats used for a particular country and is specific to a particular job and its criteria.

Now complete this part of your Personal Plan.

15.12.1   Outcome

You have now completed your Targeted Resume. It is:

● Digital, which makes it easy to change and adapt for different job applications.

● In the appropriate format for your country and region.

● Applicable to the particular job application and the job criteria.

● Appropriate for your particular career or profession.

● Follows a suitable layout for a graduate's resume.

15.12.2   Other job applications

You will repeat the above process for other job applications. Alternatively, a simpler approach is to fine tune your Targeted Resume for new job applications. This aims to ensure your Targeted Resume addresses the criteria for that job.

Different parts of your skills set are in your Foundation Resume, which you will use for different job applications.

15.13 Check: Targeted Resume

Once you have completed your draft Targeted Resume, ask someone (preferably with a professional background) to check it. You are asking for their advice on the overall presentation and content. Ask them if it comes across as:

- Professional, well-presented and succinct?

- Easy to read?

- Able to present key information about you?

- A good reflection of you, your achievements and your potential?

- Easily assessed by a potential manager and interview panel?

Review the suggestions and make any necessary changes.

15.14 Summary

This chapter has looked at different countries and regions. It has explored the different layout formats. It is clear that there is no one size fits all for any country. The focus has been to build the key content material; the rearrangement is an editing phase to adapt it to the format of the target country. Each reader will need to select an appropriate format.

At this stage you will have built the components of a resume format that is applicable to your country, region and profession.

A number of options for your resume template were provided. This included examples for Australia, New Zealand, the UK, USA, Europe, Asia, Canada, South America and China. The creation of your final resume has involved editing and copying details from your Foundation Resume into your selected Targeted Resume format.

You will end up with two valuable job search resource documents:

- Foundation Resume: a base resource of your achievements, skills and experience.
  This should be kept up to date. It is a valuable resource for all parts of job hunting through to the interview stage.
- Targeted Resume: your short job application resume, usually one to two pages. It will be targeted to a specific job and in a format appropriate to the country or job type.
  You will build progressively different versions of your Targeted Resume. This comes about as you apply for different jobs and adapt your resume to specific job criteria. Develop a good digital filing system for different documents so you retain these for future use.

You have now completed the Targeted Resume to accompany your job application.

In the next chapter, your tailored job application cover letter will be developed.

15.15   References and further reading

15.15.1   Australia and New Zealand

Graduate Careers Australia (GCA), *All About Applications*. www.graduatecareers.com.au/careerplanningandresources/preparingyour-application/allaboutapplications/ or via the short cut: https://tinyurl.com/ksf5c87

Griffith University, Queensland, *Resumes*. www.griffith.edu.au/careers-employment/get-job-ready/resumes or via the short cut: https://tinyurl.com/mssddda

Queensland University of Technology (QUT), Resume resources and examples of resumes for different faculties/professions. www.careers.qut.edu.au/student/resume.jsp or via the short cut: https://tinyurl.com/ygbsgha

Sydney University, *Resume Contents and Examples*. https://sydney.edu.au/careers/students/applying-for-jobs/how-to-write-a-resume.html or via the short cut: https://tinyurl.com/ybkthqez

University of New South Wales, *Resume Tips – Answers*. https://student.unsw.edu.au/resume-tips-answers or via the short cut: https://tinyurl.com/m27oc5n

CareersNZ is a government agency that provides assistance with job hunting. Their website contains useful resources and resume examples. www.careers.govt.nz/job-hunting/cvs-and-cover-letters/templates/#cID_500 or via the short cut: https://tinyurl.com/m7tpuc2

15.15.2 United Kingdom (UK)

CV-Library UK, *CV Templates*. www.cv-library.co.uk/cvtemplates or via the short cut: https://tinyurl.com/kuda55c

Modelo Curriculum, *The CV in the UK*. http://resume.modelocurriculum.net/the-cv-in-the-uk.html or via the short cut: https://tinyurl.com/pa9cye2

University of Kent, *Example CVs, Covering Letters and Application Forms*. www.kent.ac.uk/careers/cv/cvexamples.htm or via the short cut: https://tinyurl.com/gr9wcul

University of Manchester, *Examples of CVs for Different Jobs*. www.careers.manchester.ac.uk/applicationsinterviews/cv/examplecvs/ or via the short cut: https://tinyurl.com/oogjtcu

University of Oxford, *CVs*. www.careers.ox.ac.uk/cvs/

15.15.3 United States of America (USA)

American University, *Resumes and Curriculum Vitae (CV)*. www.american.edu/careercenter/Resumes.cfm or via the short cut: https://tinyurl.com/n86k33w

Berkeley University of California, Career Center, *International Students: Resumes – US Style*. https://career.berkeley.edu/IntnlStudents/IS-resume or via the short cut: https://tinyurl.com/muah3jq

Career One®. *Resume*. http://career-advice.careerone.com.au/resume-cover-letter/resume-writing/jobs.aspx or via the short cut: https://tinyurl.com/l55k5u9

Live Career, Free resume samples and examples. www.livecareer.com/resume-samples#include_in_resume

USAJOBS. www.usajobs.gov/

USAJOBS, *How to Build a Resume*. www.usajobs.gov/Help/how-to/account/documents/resume/build/ or via the short cut: https://tinyurl.com/ll7f6j6

15.15.4 *Europe*

Europass. http://europass.cedefop.europa.eu/

Europass, *CV – Examples*. http://europass.cedefop.europa.eu/documents/curriculum-vitae/examples or via the short cut: https://tinyurl.com/ln5gq5v

Europass, *Templates and Guidelines*. http://europass.cedefop.europa.eu/documents/curriculum-vitae/templates-instructions or via the short cut: https://tinyurl.com/mwfl47q

Modelo Curriculum, *The CV in Europe*. http://resume.modelocurriculum.net/the-cv-in-europe.html or via the short cut: https://tinyurl.com/mvl24ey

Redstar Resume Publications©. www.redstarresume.com

Resume 2017, *How Resume Format Differs Around the World*. www.resumes2017.com/how-resume-format-differs-around-the-world/ or via the short cut: https://tinyurl.com/mpyzaxj

15.15.5 *Asia*

Ashcroft, B. (2013) *Write the Perfect CV for your New Job in Asia*. Expat Job Market, 22 February. https://expatjobmarket.com/career-advice/write-the-perfect-cv-asia/ or via the short cut: https://tinyurl.com/ly7qf4l

City University of Hong Kong, Career and Leadership Centre. www6. cityu.edu.hk/caio/city-u/index.asp or via the short cut: https://tinyurl. com/kcj56kd See also: *Letters and Resumes.* www6.cityu.edu.hk/ caio/city-u/page.asp?id=13 or via the short cut: https://tinyurl.com/ kqlmmhv

JobERA, *Japan Resume and Rirekisho Writing Guide.* http://jobera.com/ japan/japan-resume-rirekisho.html or via the short cut: https://tinyurl. com/n7gewnc

Nanyang Technical University, Singapore, *Tips for an EYE-CATCHING resume!* http://ntu.jobscentral.com.sg/files/sample/ or via the short cut: https://tinyurl.com/kmyeq75

Resume Edge. www.resumeedge.com/resumes-from-around-the-world/ or via the short cut: https://tinyurl.com/kkbq5ev

15.15.6 Canada

McGill University, Montreal, Career Planning Service, *How to Write a CV.* www.mcgill.ca/caps/files/caps/guide_cv.pdf or via the short cut: https:// tinyurl.com/lkkrqmn

Moving 2 Canada, *Resume Format in Canada.* http://moving2canada. com/jobs-in-canada/resume-format-in-canada/ or via the short cut: https://tinyurl.com/kza6ano

15.15.7 South America

Going Global, *Resume/CVs.* www.goinglobal.com/guide-article-detail/ ?guide_id=1&guide_article_id=11 or via the short cut: https://tinyurl. com/km44xdw

Visual CV, *What to Include in a CV – An International Guide.* www. visualcv.com/what-to-include-in-a-cv/ or via the short cut: https:// tinyurl.com/mnnuhue

15.15.8 China

Hanbridge Mandarin. *How to Write a Chinese Resume.* www.hanbridge-mandarin.com/article/business-chinese-learning-tips/how-to-write-a-chinese-resume/ or via the short cut: https://tinyurl.com/lgovx3w

JobERA.com, *China Resume Writing Guide*. http://jobera.com/china/china-resume.html or via the short cut: https://tinyurl.com/mu8ens2

Theobald, O. (2016) *How to Prepare your Resume and Interview for Jobs in China,* Asia Options, 18 October. www.asiaoptions.org/how-to-prepare-your-resume-and-interview-to-work-in-china/ or via the short cut: https://tinyurl.com/mvpvhbm

University of Exeter, Careers and Employment, *Global Employability: Chinese CVs and Covering Letters.* www.exeter.ac.uk/media/universityofexeter/careersandemployability/globalemployability/pdfs/Chinese_CVs_and_Covering_letter_advice.pdf or via the short cut: https://tinyurl.com/lm5dltg

15.15.9 Reference: eResources link for this book

For added resources and digital files related to this chapter:

Search: Routledge Text Books or go to: www.routledge.com/

Search window: type "Your Career", which will take you to the eResources for this book.

Or via the short cut: https://tinyurl.com/kyxnfaq

Then go to either:

- Appendices <TAB> Resources <TAB> (Appendices: Resources);
- Templates <TAB> and the range of resume options;
- Appendices <TAB> Personal Plan <TAB> (Appendices: Personal Plan); or
- Web References <TAB> References <TAB>.

Preparing your tailored cover letter

16.1 Introduction

Your cover letter for a job application is a crucially important document. In this chapter, the key requirements are reviewed. It includes the importance of the letter, the need for it to be professional, as well as the need for good presentation and style. Examples of cover letters are provided in the Appendices: Resources. It needs to be tailored to specific job criteria. Presentation, style and content are addressed. You will develop your job application cover letter outline using the Personal Plan.

16.2 Cover letter: purpose

This is one of the most important parts of a job application. It can be a make or break letter. For many job openings, there can be a large number of applications. The first selection assessment of applicants is done based on the cover letter. Those that are likely prospects are passed onto the next stage for evaluation, such as checking your resume and references; those that appear to be unlikely are rejected. If the cover letter does not show relevance to the job and the job selection criteria, then it is possible that the application may be rejected at this early stage.

Cover Letter: Importance

Your cover letter needs to stand out from other applications.

16.3   Presentation and style

Presentation and Style

The cover letter must be professional, well written and concise. It must relate your application to the job and its requirements. It should attract attention for the right reasons, be visually appealing and well set out. The points made should be strong enough to identify you as a likely prospect for the position. Ideally it should help "sell you" as a contender for the job.

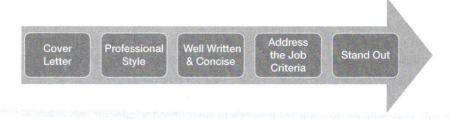

The cover letter needs to:

- indicate a strong interest in the advertised position and your experience and capabilities to undertake it;

- briefly summarise your main skills and qualifications (they can be in short sentence form or bullet points);

- have statements that link your abilities to the job criteria;

- include an extra statement to say you can make a positive contribution to the organisation;

- show interest and enthusiasm to work for the organisation; and

- welcome the opportunity for an interview for the role.

16.3.1   Cover letter components

The overall aim is to make it easy to link your capabilities to the job. You are marketing yourself to the manager and interview panel.

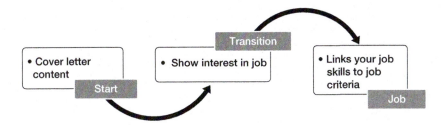

The letter preparation can be done in two stages. First, prepare a preliminary general letter. Then adapt the letter later so it is tailored to the particular job. The guidelines in this book will help you craft a good cover letter. You should adapt the cover letter to the layout and style that is the norm for your country or region.

16.4 Tailored cover letter

Tailored Cover Letter: Job Application

Once the job criteria are known, the preliminary cover letter can be tailored to the specific job. As you apply for successive jobs, you will adapt your cover letter. File them, as they can be a resource to draw on and modify in subsequent job applications.

You want to ensure your letter briefly links to the key job criteria. It is the key entrance document that links your application to the job.

16.5 Personal Plan: cover letter

The cover letter preparation comes last in the job application phase. It follows your resume, which is adapted to the particular job criteria. Identify key job criteria. Prepare any other key points for the job application. Add them into your cover letter.

Examples of general cover letters are in:

- Appendix Resources 7: cover letter example 1.
- Appendix Resources 8: cover letter example 2.

These two examples have similar content and approach, but different presentation styles. You will need to decide the most appropriate style that best presents your capabilities and application.

To download the eResource digital Appendices: Personal Plan, follow the instructions in the References at the end of the chapter.

Commence the key points for your letter in Appendix Personal Plan 15: cover letter. You now have the main components for your letter. Use it to write a general cover letter.

The digital Word examples for cover letters are downloadable via the book's eResource website.

See the References: eResource link at the end of the chapter. Once you have specific details for a job, tailor the letter to that job and its criteria.

16.6 Summary

In this chapter the basic framework for a good job application cover letter has been covered.

It includes the importance of the letter and the need for it to be professional. The importance of good presentation and style was outlined. Examples have been provided in the Appendices Resources: cover letter and the eResources website for this book.

The Personal Plan has allowed you to develop the key components of your cover letter. The cover letter should link your application to the key criteria for the job. Its aim is to take your application to the next stage and evaluation of your resume.

Each of your job applications can have a slightly modified letter that is tailored to the job and its main criteria.

In the next chapter, interview preparation will be covered.

16.7 References and further reading

Block, J.A. and Betrus, M. (1999) *101 Best Cover Letters*. (McGraw-Hill, New York, NY, USA).

Hansen, K. and Hansen, R.S. (2001) *Dynamic Cover Letters*. (Ten Speed Press, Berkeley, CA, USA).

Innes, J. (2012) *The Cover Letter Book: How to Write a Winning Cover Letter that Really Gets Noticed*. (Pearsons, Harlow, UK).

Strunk, W. and White, E.B. (2014) *The Elements of Style*. (Pearsons New International Edition, Harlow, UK).

Yate, M. (2014) *Knock 'em Dead Cover Letters: Cover Letters and Strategies to Get the Job You Want*. (Adams Media, Avon, MA, USA).

16.7.1 Reference: eResources link for this book

For added resources and digital files related to this chapter:

Search: Routledge Text Books or go to: www.routledge.com/

Search window: type "Your Career", which will it take you to the eResources for this book.

Or via the short cut:https://tinyurl.com/kyxnfaq

Then go to either:

- Appendices <TAB> Resources <TAB> (Appendices: Resources);
- Templates <TAB> Cover Letter <TAB>;
- Appendices <TAB> Personal Plan <TAB> (Appendices: Personal Plan).

17 | Interviews

17.1 Introduction

This chapter is about preparing for your interviews. For most people, interviews are generally a rare or occasional experience. If you are job hunting in a competitive market and you succeeded in reaching the interview stage, they are more frequent. It is important to know your "selling points" and use them in responses to interview questions.

You have already prepared them in your achievement statements. They are in:

● Appendix Personal Plan 10: General Achievements.
● Appendix Personal Plan 11: Achievements Extended.

You Foundation Resume contains valuable material for your interview preparation. You developed the key points via your Personal Plan:

● Appendix Personal Plan 12: Foundation Resume – stage 1.
● Appendix Personal Plan 13: Foundation Resume – stage 2.

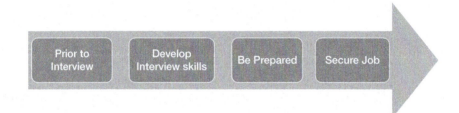

Prior to Interview | Develop Interview skills | Be Prepared | Secure Job

Interview skills are important for securing a new job. It includes "body language" communication. It is important to prepare responses for possible questions. Use role play practice before being interviewed.

Dress and presentation techniques will be covered. The use of online techniques such as Skype for video interviews will increase. An outline of the preparations needed for an interview via Skype will be given.

17.2 Job selection psychology: review

It is important to recognise and understand the psychology of why managers employ a particular person for a vacancy. What motivates them or influences their decision? Is it the highest qualifications? Is it the best experience? Or, is it the person with people skills who can present themselves well? Is it a person who will assist them to do their job?

We want you to understand all these factors so you can use them to help you win the job.

Understand Job Selection Psychology

There is a deeper psychological reason why a manager employs a person. It is based on the key question, will the potential employee help the manager to:

- do his or her work better?
- support the manager's goals (these may be personal goals or work assigned performance targets)?
- make the organisation or business successful?
- overcome problems and challenges the manager is facing?

How can you respond to these deeper psychological motivations? It can be done easily by preparing (in writing) and practising short "helping statements" that respond to these needs. These short statements can be selectively added to your interview responses.

In response to a question about your qualifications you could reply by simply listing them. Alternatively, you can list them and add a "helping statement". For example: "my qualifications are (...), which I believe will help you manage (example activity)."

Some example "helping statements" are:

- (response), which can assist you to meet your goals.
- (response), which will contribute to the organisation.
- (response), which will help meet work targets.

In Chapter 4: Job hunting – key factors, we explored this topic. In your Personal Plan (Appendix Personal Plan 4: job selection psychology) you created your "helping statements". These recognise the needs of the manager. They show that you are interested in helping the manager to meet his or her needs. Learn them and add them into your responses in an interview.

17.3   Interview preparation

17.3.1   Web: potential employer information

The Internet or web is a great resource for interview preparation. Check potential employers' websites. Explore their programmes and their value statements. Use it to gain an understanding of the potential employer organisation.

It will assist you in the interview. It can show the interview panel that you are thorough, do your homework and research well. These are all positive added ticks for your application.

17.3.2   Other sources of information

17.3.2.1   Colleagues

Do you have colleagues or friends already in the workforce or profession? If so, consider asking for their advice as part of your interview preparation. It may provide useful information from someone who has already been through the job hunting process. The key questions are:

- What are the key things to do to prepare for an interview?
- What tips and suggestions do you have?

17.3.2.2   Mentors in your profession

These can be a valuable asset as you move from being an under-graduate to a professional job. They can assist you through guidance and helpful job hunting advice. Most people value recognition and the fact you are asking for their advice is a positive reflection of that recognition. Professionals are usually busy people, so it is important that your approach recognises that their time is limited; perhaps asking for just 15 minutes of their valuable time may be worthwhile initially.

17.3.2.3   Mentors in other professions

These can be a valuable support. If involved in personnel selection they may be able to help with the interview phase. The job interview and selection processes are common to most professions. Seek out people to guide you in your preparation. Your aim is to ask for their help, to listen and use it to prepare yourself.

17.3.3   Questions: job interview preparation

What sort of questions will you face in the interview? Some people are capable of handling new questions "on the run" and providing good responses; however, for the majority, preparation and practice are needed.

The more you prepare and practise via role-plays the better your responses will be to questions. This will increase your chances of success.

Questions: Job Interview Preparation

The first aim is to research potential questions. Ask colleagues, friends, mentors or other professionals about the common questions. Check through the job criteria as this is another key source for questions. Each criterion may represent several questions on that topic. Use these to frame associated questions. From the full list of questions, brainstorm key points for your answers. Then edit and mould these into short responses to fully address the question. Check your approach with a mentor or another professional. Modify them if necessary.

Use the achievement statements you have already completed in your Personal Plan:

- Appendix Personal Plan 10: General Achievements.
- Appendix Personal Plan 11: Achievements Extended.

They are a valuable resource in preparing for your interview and responses.

Your Foundation Resume is another valuable resource for interview preparation.

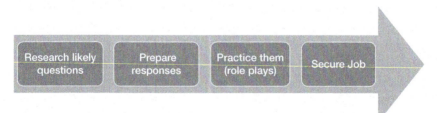

You can also prepare for possible general questions that could be part of the interview:

- What are your valuable abilities?
- What are your main personal characteristics?
- What values underpin your approach to work (or life)?

17.3.4   Your unique selling points

These are the things that make you stand out from others. They flow from your education, life experience, personal characteristics and values. Your achievements (or "selling points") were developed in your Personal Plan (Appendices: Personal Plans 10 and 11).

For each topic (e.g. teamwork), you developed two or three short sentences or bullet points. These summarise your achievements and they become personal "selling points". They covered areas such as quality, people skills, customer service and communication.

Review them as you prepare your short responses to possible questions. Edit them and practise them with a friend or colleague in role plays for an interview.

17.3.5   Role plays

Use Role Plays to Practice for Interviews

There is a saying that says "practise makes perfect". As with any skill in life we need to understand it, learn it and apply it through practise. After you have completed this interview preparation chapter, seek out a family member, friend or colleague. Ask them to help you to role play for an interview. They play the role of the interviewer. They can ask the questions you have already prepared. You can then respond with your answers, achievements and personal selling points. These are the responses you have already written out as part of your preparation.

Ask your role play partner to provide both positive and negative feedback. Repeat this and keep practising and improving. Your confidence increases as your skills in the interview setting develop.

| Use Role Plays | ➡ | Develop Interview Skills | ➡ | Practise Them |

17.3.6   Interview panel

In most cases, it is unlikely that you will know who will be on the interview panel. For smaller organisations, the interviewer may be the manager. For larger organisations and government bodies, the panel could be three people. The interview could be conducted by the manager where there is a vacancy, a human resource person and someone from a related section to provide an independent perspective.

When invited for an interview, thank them for the opportunity. It is also reasonable to ask "what is the structure for the interview?" It is not essential, but removes any surprises as you walk into the interview. Preparation can lead to a more relaxed approach and better responses.

17.3.7 Communication: body language

Communication: Learn Body Language

Good communication is a great skill. We use communication all the time, but do we really know the art of successful communication? It is important to know the positive skills for good communication; it can help you get the job you are seeking.

The first part is written communication skills, such as a strong cover letter and a good resume. The second part covers personal communication skills and interaction with the interview panel.

Psychology teaches that real communication is made up of three parts:

- What we say (content).
- How we say it (tone).
- How we convey it (body language).

Some studies have assessed the contributions of these three different parts. Surprisingly, content (words) only represents around 7% of a message; tone and voice represent 38% of the message; and body language represents around 55% of a message. So knowing about body language and using voice tone is crucial for good communication.

Words = 7% of Message
Tone and Voice = 38% of Message
Body Language = 55% of Message

While the percentage influence of words versus body language may be debated, it is evident that body language conveys a significant part of the message.

See Mehrabian (1972), Yaffe (2011) and Leading Personality (blog) in the References at the end of this chapter.

Carter et al. (2015) remind us that "It's what you don't say that counts." In other words the messages we really send are more about our voice, tone and body language than the words we say.

Our words may say one thing, but our body language and voice tone may be saying the opposite. It is the body language that others pick up on. It is usually the real message. Therefore, it is important to learn about the keys to communication and it is at the centre of most things we do.

By learning these skills, understanding them and applying them, you will have increased your chances of winning a job. Sometimes it is hard to look at ourselves, so seek feedback from friends or colleagues on your communication skills as you practise role plays for interviews. Ask for feedback on your tone and body language as to how are you coming across.

17.3.7.1 Posture

Posture in the interview is closely related to body language. There is a widely used acronym that can help you learn body posture and body language skills. It was devised by Egan (1986) and it is known as S-O-L-E-R:

S   Sit **square** onto the person who is asking questions. Sitting at an angle to the person you are talking to can be seen as evasive or less in contact.

O   Be **open** in your posture. Your arms should not be crossed as this conveys a "closed" message. Your posture should express a willingness to engage with the other person.

L   **Lean forward**. This shows you are interested and indicates your attention is on the person you are communicating with. It shows that you are engaged.

E   **Eye contact** is important. This is especially so in Western countries, as it reflects a personal engagement with the other person. In a job interview, the other person is the manager or a member of the interview panel. In some cultures, for example India, lowered eyes and less eye contact is often the norm; it can reflect acknowledgement of a more senior person. Clearly, different body language norms apply in different cultures.

R   **Responsive**. Your words, posture and body language can all be used to convey a responsive manner. Seek feedback on how well you are doing from your role play partner.

Body Language: Remember S-O-L-E-R

Overall, your posture seeks to convey openness, responsiveness and interest to the manager or members of the interview panel. Practise these skills and use them in your interview. This is important.

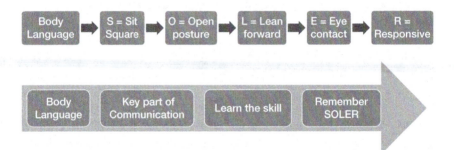

17.3.8   Initial interview meeting

It is important to realise that others usually assess us in the first minute of contact. Therefore, when you walk into an interview room it is important that you make a positive impression on the interview panel.

Learn and practise greeting skills. A firm handshake and "I am pleased to meet you" is usually sufficient. It needs to be coupled with positive eye contact and positive body language. These are all important parts of good communication.

17.3.9   End of interview contact

Use the end of the interview to project a positive image. It is about a firm handshake and a thank you for the opportunity for the interview. It is an opportunity to say "I look forward to the results. I would welcome the opportunity to work for this organisation".

17.3.10 Dress and personal presentation

This is important preparation for a job interview. It is about knowing what is appropriate and what is not in terms of dress sense. Your dress and clothing choice conveys a message of who you are and possibly the type of person you may be as a potential employee.

Do you look smart, well-dressed and professional? Do you look unkempt (poor hairstyle), with bad make up or inappropriately dressed? Is your outfit or clothing too casual or unsuitable?

Personal Presentation is Important

Do you have body art (body piercings, rings or tattoos)? You need to look at these things from the perspective of other people. Your interviewer may be from a different generation and have quite different perspectives to you. They may be considering how you may affect the organisation's potential clients. It is important to realise they may come from different generations and have different value systems. Each generation has its own ways of assessing body art. Body art is a form of communication; to some people it can convey a message that is negative.

Nose piercings can be significant for some people. What image do they project of you in terms of this job? In most cases they can be removed. What is the alternative image that other applicants may be projecting?

Tattoos cannot be removed, but may be covered up by wearing long sleeves. The choice is ultimately yours. It is about recognising that our appearance and body language is part of the communication message we convey to others about ourselves.

Check Your Personal Presentation

17.3.11 Online interviews: Skype

Skype is a free communication tool that uses the Internet. It provides online conversation (with voice and real-time video) between the participants. It allows interactive discussions, questions and responses with accompanying images of you and the person(s) on the other end. Each party can see the other, plus their own image is also visible in a smaller screen box.

Tools such as Skype allow interviews to be conducted online on PCs and mobile devices. This can be more convenient for applicants and more cost-effective considering travel times and costs for employers. Skype interviews are an invaluable tool for initial screening and selection of potential candidates.

Video cameras and speakers are built into new laptops. For computers without them, you can easily add a web camera with a built in microphone.

You will need to download Skype and get a Skype username. For set-up instructions just follow the Skype guidelines. These will allow you to check the audio and your image (from the webcam). There is no direct added cost, as Skype uses the Internet for the communication and this is irrespective of the distance or different locations.

The presentation techniques outlined for face-to-face interviews largely apply for Skype interviewing as well.

Plan for Your Skype Interview

Mark Feffer provides advice on how to succeed in your Skype interview. He advises that the key to a successful Skype conversation is planning. This means sorting out all the technical issues involved with a Skype link. Test it out and be prepared.

17.3.11.1 Preparation

Some key tips from Feffer on how to make sure you are ready include:

- Set up ahead of time. Check your Skype well before the interview is scheduled.
- Test it out with friends.
- Check your camera orientation so your face is nicely framed.
- Test your microphone. Ensure the microphone you are using delivers good sound.
- Check the room lighting to make sure your Skype screen image is not too bright or too dark.

- If you wear glasses, check and minimise light reflection of the lenses by changing the angle of the camera or your position.

- Set up the room so it looks professional.

Rehearse Your Interview

17.3.11.2 Rehearse

Practise will make you more comfortable using Skype for an interview. Mistakes to avoid include watching the monitor and your screen image, which results in a head down negative appearance. You need to practise looking up and looking at the web camera. This way you are looking at the person on the other end of the interview. Find a comfortable position.

Do trial Skype interviews with your friends. Practise will make your interview come across as smooth and professional.

See Feffer, 5 *Tips to Ace Your Skype Job Interview*, in the References at the end of this chapter. Other factors to include in your preparation and rehearsal include:

- Interview environment: make sure it is a good quiet setting, free from possible disturbance.

- Presentation: dress professionally as you would do for a face-to-face interview.

- Body language: follow the body language techniques outlined earlier. Remember the acronym S-O-L-E-R. Focus on looking at the web camera and not on the monitor screen. You can practise getting this right with your trial Skype interview with a friend. A large part of your communicated message comes from your body language and your tone.

17.4 Interviews: experts' advice

Firestone's (2014) *Ultimate Guide to Job Interview – Answers* is a valuable and informative book. A summary of key points has been included in Appendix Resources 9: Interviews – expert's advice.

In it, Firestone has identified the main themes or goals of interview questions. He has identified 40 competencies (i.e. achievements) and groups them under themes that are related to interview question areas.

He uses S-O-A-R-L as an acronym to develop the achievement statements. This represents Situation - Objective - Action - Results - Learning approach.

This is another way to create your achievement statements for key themes (e.g. teamwork).

These can be used for your resume and interview responses.

Interview Skills

Firestone's book helps you prepare for an interview and provides responses for a wide range of interview questions. See the Appendix Resources 9: Interviews – expert's advice, for key points on:

- The fundamental interview questions.
- Behavioural interview approach.
- Creating achievement statements (i.e. competencies).
- Main behavioural competencies.
- Key interview questions.
- Yes and no questions.
- Questions you can ask.
- Closing statement.

17.5 Interview or job application rejection: moving forward

17.5.1 Surviving rejections

Interviews are something most people usually have little experience of doing. The chance of making mistakes is naturally higher when doing something we are not familiar with. Add in the pressure and hopes associated with the interview, the thoughts about the types of questions and how you might respond and it all adds up to a hard environment.

Interview rejections are an unfortunate but real part of job hunting. How can you overcome the impact of rejections and keep moving forward?

You Can Move on from Interview Rejections

Uzair Bawany (2011), from *The Guardian Jobs*, advises on how to survive rejection:

- Do not let rejections dent your confidence. Move on from doubts. Treat interviews as a learning experience and grow in experience. The right job will come.
- Develop resilience and find ways to improve your interview technique.
- Fine tune your responses so you present better answers.
- Try and get post-interview feedback on how you interviewed.

We all understand that dealing with rejection in job hunting can be difficult. The key is staying positive and avoiding feeling depressed. It is understandable to feel down, but the challenge is working your way through it. Keep persevering and put it behind you. Do not take it personally. It does not diminish your value as person, which continues.

So how do you survive and move forward?

Majumder offers *Nine Tips to Deal with Job Search Rejection*. Broadly, the key messages are:

- Allow for Plan B: do not pin your hopes on one specific job. Pursue multiple opportunities.
- Interviews are not professional validations; they are about meeting the employers' needs, not yours.
- Seek feedback: any feedback, even negative is worthwhile. Accept the rejection and move on. Do not get into the self-blame game as it will just drag you down.
- Focus on positives: avoid reliving negative interviews. Focus on the positives and successes in your life.
- Concentrate on your strengths: do not beat yourself up just because you have been rejected. Try and focus on your strengths; identify opportunities that you are enthusiastic about. It comes through in interviews.

- Realise you are not alone: many more people are turned down for jobs than land them. Once you accept that, you can explore the next opportunity.

- Keep a positive attitude: the best way to deal with rejections is to keep smiling. Look ahead to the day you will find that job.

Career One, *How to Deal with Rejection,* has identified key tips from recruitment specialists on how to deal with rejection:

- Know that rejection is a normal part of job hunting.

- Reduce stress by exercising regularly.

- Partner with a recruitment expert for advice.

- Be positive and be persistent. Do not lose hope as there is a job out there.

- View rejection as a lack of fit between you and the particular job.

- Approach your next application with renewed enthusiasm and confidence in your abilities.

- Keep refining and improving your resume and your interview technique.

17.5.2 *Personal factors*

Rejections can be tough and challenging; they can be spiritually and mentally draining. It is important to develop techniques to lift your spirit and keep encouraging yourself.

In Chapter 3: Personal factors, we focused on you the person. This is important particularly after you have had a rejection. It is worthwhile reviewing that chapter. Some of the key aspects are summarised below.

Develop personal skills such as:

- Resilience: this is the ability to bounce back after setbacks or disappointments. Surprisingly, people can grow from setbacks and failures; the personal growth from tough times provides added strength to cope with life and its challenges. Treat setbacks as an opportunity to learn and to bounce back.

- Endurance: this is the ability to keep going. It is about recognising that the job hunt is often more a marathon race than a sprint. Endurance can be both mental and spiritual.

- Adaptability: this is the ability to change and accommodate changing circumstances (similar to a chameleon). In a rapidly changing world, it is a valuable trait to develop. For some people, it comes naturally; for others, they may need to work to develop it. The changes in types of employment and the rate of change are increasing. Economies change, employment markets change and skill requirements from employers change. It has been suggested that many in today's generation will have six or more careers on average in their lifetime. That is not just different jobs, but different roles and careers. This will require adaptability to handle the change.

17.5.3   Conditioning our thinking

Build up techniques for positive thinking. Those with spiritual beliefs can draw on their faith, spiritual encouragement or wisdom literature. This can encourage and assist you to last the distance when the going seems tough.

17.5.3.1   Spirit lifters

These are positive affirmations that can lift our souls when we are feeling overburdened. The positive words can sooth us and encourage us. The small negative inner voice that sows doubts can be troubling. As you learn to recognise it and respond with positive affirmations you can move from the negative to the positive. Spiritual material and wisdom literature can be powerful.

17.5.3.2   Thought conditioners

Just as we can do gym work to develop our bodies, using thought conditioners provide a similar workout for our spirit. They can help people build up their spirit and their souls. Negative thought patterns can overwhelm us or make us less able to function. Thought conditioners can help overcome negative thought patterns that can drag us down. They can help us develop positive thought patterns.

17.5.4 Support from family and friends

Find people who you can call on to provide support and encouragement. A supportive friend or family member and a listening ear can do wonders. Just by sharing your worries with a family member or friend, is like sharing the burden. It helps you regain a clearer perspective and move to the next opportunity. Call on family and friends for support.

17.6 Summary

Learn the techniques for good interviewing. Prepare for the interview. Get advice. Develop potential interview questions and practise them in an interview role play setting with a friend or colleague. Go back over your achievement statements that you developed in your Personal Plan. These are well-prepared short punchy responses to key job criteria. They are just right for an interview. It is better to use these than to try longer and possibly more rambling responses to questions off the cuff.

Recognise the employer's deeper needs, which is to have a person that will help him or her meet their goals. Practise the "helping statements" that you can periodically add to your responses. Develop your body language communication skills and get feedback from a friend on how you are doing.

Be prepared and practise if you need to do a Skype interview. Complete the interview preparation outlined in this chapter well before an actual interview. This will give you more time to fine tune your interview skills. If you leave it until you get an interview, it is often too late to do it properly, prepare and practise.

The interview is a key stage. It is your chance to shine and employ positive interview techniques. These increase your chances of appointment to a new job. It is about hard work and preparation more than good luck. The fact you are reading this book shows you are taking job hunting seriously.

Interview and job rejections are something that happen to many people and are a part of the job selection process. Only one person can be selected for a job. Many others, including you, may have been passed over. You are still the same valuable person. Understandably, you will feel disappointment, but your inner value is not diminished. Move on to the next application.

Build up your resilience and endurance. Learn from the interviews and move forward.

Keep your spirits up.

The next chapter is the conclusion and provides an overview of job search preparation and job hunting.

17.7 References and further reading

Bawany, U. (2011) Didn't get the job? How to survive rejection. *The Guardian Jobs*, 12 August. https://jobs.theguardian.com/article/didn-t-get-the-job-how-to-survive-rejection/ or via the short cut: https://tiny-url.com/mdpb6oq

Career Confidential. www.CareerConfidential.com

Career Confidential, *Job Interview Q&A*. Google Play. https://play.google.com/store/apps/details?id = com.careerconfidential.jobqa&hl = en or via the short cut: https://tinyurl.com/p57wbtn

Career One, *How to Deal with Rejection*. www.careerone.com.au/watercoolertalk/job-hunting/graduates/how-to-deal-with-rejection or via the short cut: https://tinyurl.com/lqm4oq4

Carter, C., Walbridge, D. and Zimmerman, F. (2015) *Student Body Language*. (Carter Entertainment, Kindle edn).

Egan, G. (1986) *The Skilled Helper*. (Brooks/Cole, Belmont, CA, 3rd edn).

Feffer, M., *5 Tips to Ace Your Skype Job Interview*. Job Hunt. www.job-hunt.org/IT-job-search/skype-job-interview.shtml or via the short cut: https://tinyurl.com/h4mxldq

Firestone, B. (2014) *Ultimate Guide to Job Interview – Answers* (Success Patterns, Santa Monica, CA, 7th edn).

Leading Personality. Wordpress, https://leadingpersonality.wordpress.com/2013/05/28/read-body-language-signs-and-gestures/

Majumder, S., *Nine Tips to Deal with Job Search Rejection*. CareerCast. www.careercast.com/career-news/nine-tips-deal-job-search-rejection or via the short cut: https://tinyurl.com/k36gf3x

McKee, P. (2012) *How to Answer Interview Questions*. (CareerConfidential, Paden, Oklahoma, USA).

Mehrabian, A. (1972) *Silent Messages*. (Wadsworth Publishing, Belmont, CA, USA).

Yaffe, P. (2011) The 7% rule fact, fiction, or misunderstanding. (*Ubiquity*, Vol. 2011, October 2011, DOI: 10.1145/2043155.2043156).

17.7.1   Reference: eResources link for this book

For added resources and digital files related to this chapter:

Search: Routledge Text Books or go to: www.routledge.com/

Search window: type "Your Career", which will it take you to the eResources for this book. Or via the short cut: https://tinyurl.com/kyxnfaq

Then go to:

- Appendices <TAB> Resources <TAB> (Appendices: Resources).

Conclusion
Job search preparation and job hunting

18.1 Introduction

This final chapter highlights the main stages to help you win that first job. The approach used in the book has been to help you break down the large and potentially overwhelming activity of job searching, such as writing a resume, cover letter, interviewing techniques, etc., into smaller, more manageable parts. Each part is further segmented so that students can go back to an earlier part and review it. In this way, we have shown you how to build up an impressive resume, write a winning cover letter and know where to search for jobs. It includes tips on how to use social media for job hunting.

18.2 Conclusion: job search preparation

Prepare for the Job Search

One aim of the book is to maximise the personal benefits for the reader. The Appendices: Personal Plan tailor the material to the reader's personal needs. We trust you have completed each part as you progressed through the chapters. The aim has been to convert advice into action that relates to you. Your Personal Plan provides valuable preparation for your job hunt.

Build Your Personal Plan to Secure a Job

The Appendices: Resources have provided sample material to draw on. Resumes and cover letters vary between countries. The content is frequently similar, but presented in varying ways. The main focus throughout has been on the content. Once it has been prepared, you can easily adapt it to alternate formats and layouts.

Use the Resources in the Appendices

The eResources on Routledge's website for the book has been developed to help you in your job search. It provides valuable extra resource material for readers. These include: Appendices, Resources and Templates as digital files in downloadable formats.

Use the eResources Website

In particular, readers are able to download the Appendices: Personal Plan layout in digital Word format. Completing the Personal Plan in digital format offers benefits. They become a valuable resource that can easily be copied into your Foundation Resume.

The eResources provide access to examples and templates for your resume/CV and cover letter. These can be downloaded in Word format to assist you in compiling your job application materials.

The whole process may have seemed daunting, but by breaking it up into smaller steps, you have progressed through it. We have prepared you for the challenges ahead and encouraged you to take one step at a time. This avoids being overwhelmed by the size of the project. Small steps add up to major achievements.

As job markets are changing and opportunities with them it is important to be adaptable. At times it may be necessary to rebrand yourself. Recognising your skills and achievements and then relating them to other job areas can open up new opportunities for work.

Building personal skills such as endurance, resilience and adaptability are valuable; this is because job hunting can be a long and at times emotionally demanding journey (particularly when the job market is depressed). It can be demoralising to get a rejection letter, but it is important to keep your spirit positive and to keep moving forward. Ways to keep a positive outlook, to lift your thoughts and spirits on this journey are provided to help you persevere.

The role of mentors, friends and family can help you on your journey. Sharing with others and seeking their support is encouraged; it can make the job search process much easier. It will help you overcome the hurdles that are part of job hunting.

18.3   Conclusion: job hunting

This book aims to develop your skills for getting a job and help you identify outside agencies that can assist you.

Develop Job Hunting Skills

Understanding how to locate job opportunities is important. It could be valuable to revisit Chapter 5: Locating job opportunities. The more areas of opportunity you can explore, the more chance you will have of finding a job. It is also about focusing your efforts on job market areas that offer you the best potential.

The role of social media has become a key aspect of job searching. It has been covered in:

- Chapter 6: Social media – job search options.
- Chapter 7: Social media – establishing your online profile.
- Chapter 8: Social media for job hunting.

The book has explored some of the main social media platforms such as LinkedIn, Facebook, Google Plus and Twitter for job hunting. You can choose other relevant social media platforms that are prominent in your country. Establishing your online profile (bio) is important.

Chapter 9: Personal development introduced the concept of understanding yourself. It provides support and encouragement. Often you will encounter complex choices and options as you look at many job search options. Three decision-making tools have been provided to assist you to weigh up the pros and cons of alternative options. Rather than trying to sort out complex factors by gut feeling, they can help you make sounder decisions.

The use of services that will help you evaluate your career options can be a valuable investment. The surveys on which they are based help you understand yourself, your particular skills and how these relate to different job types.

Sometimes, graduates may feel they have little experience to present in their resume. The book helps you recognise your achievements that come from your wider life experiences. The chapters on achievements and the corresponding Personal Plan help you identify your achievements and express them in short statements. These are useful for your resume and for your job interview. You have done the preparation so responding to job criteria or interview questions becomes easier.

You have addressed general achievements such as teamwork, communication, customer service, timeliness and quality. You have also addressed your achievements in relation to your chosen profession and specific job requirements as part of your extended achievements.

The work you completed in your Personal Plan provides valuable input into your Foundation Resume. It should be considered as more than a job application resume. It is a resource to draw on that contains a wealth of information about you. It is easily adapted to a specific job resume. It is a valuable resource for interviews.

The value of references and referees to support job applications was covered in Chapter 14. The ways these can be managed are outlined. The advice will help you choose referees that will enhance your chances of winning the job.

Different countries have different resume formats. For this reason, the main focus is on building up content, which has been the basis of the Foundation Resume. Your Personal Plan provides the base material for your Foundation Resume, tailored job application cover letter and your social media online profile (bio).

The context, culture and perspectives of the book are initially Western; however, it has been written in a way that can be applied across cultures. It focuses on the main principles.

Different countries, employers and cultures will have variations in job application methods and interview approaches; however, the basic principles are often common. It is up to the graduate to adapt them to make any necessary cultural or contextual changes and to relate the guidance in his book to their cultural situation and employment environment. These aspects have been explained and illustrated in Chapter 15: Preparing your targeted resume: country-specific, and in the related Appendices: Resources examples. Resume layouts for different countries and regions are reviewed. This is to help you revise your resume to the targeted country and the most commonly used format for that region.

Adapting your resume to a particular country or region is about editing the material you have already complied. The output is an accepted resume format for the region where you are applying for the job. This is your Targeted Resume.

Your job application cover letter is very important. The book shows you the key components of a good letter. Some adaption is left to the reader for contextual variations as the cover letter must be related to the particular job. This was covered in Chapter 16: Preparing your tailored cover letter. A good letter and its associated resume helps you move to the important interview stage. Developing sound skills for job interviews is important. These have been covered in Chapter 17: Interviews. Preparing and revising your achievements (and "selling points") was emphasised. Interview practice via role plays helps build skills and improves your responses. Body language skills and presentation tips were included, along with advice from experts. The aim is to increase your ability to make a positive impression on the interview panel and win the job.

It is important to regularly review your job application material. Be willing to tailor it to a specific job. You will end up with a number of slightly different resumes and cover letters. They have all evolved from your Foundation Resume and cover letter.

18.4   Your career journey: best wishes

You are on a journey from university (or tertiary course) to your first career-related job.

This is a challenging time for new graduates. This book is a resource to guide you.

The aim of the book is to help graduate students acquire the skills for job search preparation and successfully secure a job. The approach has been a step-by-step guide. It transfers the book's material into your Personal Plan for job searching. Progressively, you have built the components you will need: an understanding of the job market, your resume and cover letter, through to online social media options and interview skills. The final stage is to apply the interview skills and, it is hoped, receive a job offer.

Moving from tertiary studies with a degree or diploma is a wonderful achievement.

Best Wishes in Your New Career

Good Luck in Winning That Job!

Together, we believe the book will help you make a successful transition from university to your chosen career.

Good luck as you put them into practice and move towards the job you are seeking.

We wish you well and a successful career.

Lee Smith and John van Genderen

Appendix
Resources 1
Myers-Briggs Type
Indicator® (MBTI®)

This resource relates to Chapter 9: Personal development and is intended to be a brief overview.

The purpose of the Myers-Briggs Type Indicator® (MBTI®) personality inventory is to:

- apply the theory of psychological types described by C. G. Jung; and
- make it understandable and useful in people's lives.

It is based on the concept that apparent random variations in behaviour are actually quite orderly and consistent. The reason is explained by the differences in the ways individuals prefer to see the world, the way they process information, the basis for their decisions and how they deal with the world.

The approach identifies four basic preferences. It describes 16 distinctive personality types that flow from the interactions among the basic preferences.

See the *MBTI® Manual: A Guide to the Development and Use of the Myers-Briggs Type Indicator®* in the References at the end of this Appendix.

- Favourite world: Do you prefer to focus on the outer world or on your own inner world? This is called extraversion (E) or introversion (I).
- Information: Do you prefer to focus on the basic information you take in or do you prefer to interpret and add meaning? This is called sensing (S) or intuition (N).

- Decisions: When making decisions, do you prefer to look first at logic and consistency or to look first at the people and special circumstances? This is called thinking (T) or feeling (F).

- Structure: In dealing with the outside world, do you prefer to get things decided or do you prefer to stay open to new information and options? This is called judging (J) or perceiving (P).

Your personality type: When you decide on your preference in each category, you have your own personality type, which can be expressed as a code with four letters. There are 16 personality types of the Myers-Briggs Type Indicator® and each personality type is described by a combination of the four basic preferences; for example, ESFP or INTJ.

All types are equal, the goal of knowing about personality type is to understand and appreciate differences between people. As all types are equal, there is no best type.

The assessment provides an insight into our personalities. From this understanding it allows people to understand how they like to communicate and interact with others.

An MBTI® report provides your preference for each of four pairs:

- Extraversion (E) or introversion (I).

- Sensing (S) or intuition (N).

- Thinking (T) or feeling (F).

- Judging (J) or perceiving (P).

The assessment aims to assist you in understanding yourself as well as others.

See the *MBTI® Manual: A Guide to the Development and Use of the Myers-Briggs Type Indicator®* in the References at the end of this Appendix.

MBTI® tests are offered widely in many countries. They can also be undertaken online.

"Although popular in the business sector, the MBTI® can exhibit significant psychometric deficiencies, notably including poor validity and reliability."

See Wikipedia. Myers-Briggs, in the References at the end of this Appendix.

Some organisations have established links between MBTI® and characteristics of different jobs and careers. These can be used as a broad guide to help establish your fit to various careers. Each person is unique, so it cannot be definitive.

Some include Strong Interest Inventory® (SII) tests to help assist you to identify your interests and preferences. It is all about using tools that can help us understand ourselves. This can assist us to make good choices that fit our personalities and interests. Use the web to find organisations that may provide this online service.

See the Strong Interest Inventory in the References at the end of this Appendix.

MBTI® and SII® are two surveys or inventories. They may assist you in understanding yourself and how you interact with others.

References

Grutter, J. and Hammer, L. *Strong and MBTI® Career Report*, CPP. Online career assessment example. www.cpp.com/en/strongproducts.aspx? pc=158 or via the short cut: https://tinyurl.com/ledvr3z

MBTI® Manual: A Guide to the Development and Use of the Myers-Briggs Type Indicator®. www.myersbriggs.org/my-mbti-personality-type/mbti-basics/ or via the short cut: https://tinyurl.com/2yhr4l

MTD Training (2013) *Personal Confidence & Motivation*. Bookboon.com, ebook, http://bookboon.com/en/personal-confidence-and-motivation-ebook or via the short cut: https://tinyurl.com/y8924538

Wikipedia. Myers-Briggs. https://en.wikipedia.org/wiki/Myers%E2%80%93Briggs_Type_Indicator or via the short cut: https://tinyurl.com/odcrvvn

Appendix Resources 2

Career assessment reports

This appendix relates to Chapter 9: Personal development.

The purpose is to be a short introduction to the online career assessment reports and services that are available. The appendix outlines the broad contents that are provided via Myers-Briggs® and Strong Interest Inventory® assessments and reports as an example.

How the Strong Interest Inventory® can help

- Identify your interests.
- Identify careers and positions linked to your interests.
- Understand your preferred work types and environments.

How the report is organised

- Occupational themes: your interests, skills and values in six broad areas: realistic, investigative, artistic, social, enterprising and conventional.
- Interests: your interests associated with the occupation themes. It highlights those likely to be the most rewarding and motivating.
- Occupational scales: your likes and dislikes along with compatible occupations.
- Personal style scales: preferences for areas such as work style, teamwork, etc. and the environments that fit you best.
- Summary: profile and responses – overview of your options and interests linked to different careers.

Occupational themes: Identifies broad interest patterns under six themes.

From the survey, your score and interest level for each theme is presented. It identifies your highest themes for interest. It provides a guide to broad work categories.

Basic interest scales: Identifies specific interests that are motivating for you. These are listed in broad career and work categories; for example, mathematics or sales.

Occupational scales: identifies the occupations most closely linked with your interests. These are occupation groups you may want to explore (e.g. actuary, accountant or financial analysis). The report opens up the wide range of jobs that can be associated with your interests. Likewise, it reveals jobs that do not fit your interests.

Online links are available to further explore and learn more about the identified occupations.

Personal style scales: Reflects working and learning styles linked to your preferences. It can reflect whether you prefer to work alone or as part of a team; your risk taking profile; and your leadership style. These can guide you to different career and job areas.

Profile summary: Identifies your top interest areas and occupations based on your interest assessment.

Career assessment: Myers-Briggs (MBTI)® and Strong (SII)® evaluations

Some online career assessment reports provide a combined evaluation based on MBTI® and SII® surveys. The aim is to relate your interests and personality to different work environments that would be a good fit.

How the report is organised

- Summary of SII® and MBTI® results.
- Your preferences (SII® and MBTI® combined).
- Your personality style.
- Career fields and occupations linked to results.
- Other occupations to explore.
- Career development options.

Occupational themes: Identifies your main occupational themes based on your interests. These are drawn from six categories: realistic, investigative, artistic, social, enterprising and conventional.

It identifies your MBTI® personality type and preferences. These are based on the following personality categories:

- Your perspective: extraversion (E) or introversion (I).
- Your information style: sensing (S) or intuition (N).
- Your decision-making style: thinking (T) or feeling (F).
- Dealing with the world: judging (J) or perceiving (P).

The assessment identifies your dominant preference styles. For example, an ESFP personality type would have characteristics that include:

- Extrovert (E) activities.
- Taking in information by sensing (S).
- Making decisions by values and feelings (F).
- Dealing with the world by perception (P).

This provides a link to broad work styles that are associated with your personality type.

Your preferences (SII® and MBTI® combined)

Your preferences identify your main occupational themes based on your interests. For example, this may indicate your interests are related to conventional occupation themes such as accounting or data processing.

The MBTI® assessment will link your personality to preferences (linked to occupation styles). For example, an ESFP personality may be more attuned to hands-on solutions; responding to crises; prefer a person-centred approach and consider others' values as well as their own.

The two assessments combined can help identify:

- What type of work you like.
- Where you may like to work.
- How you prefer to work and learn.

It identifies your preferred interest area and your personality type. This is expressed in terms of work environment, how you work and what you like. For example your assessment as Conventional and ESFP may show you are suited to: interacting with others, applying past learning, attentive to facts and adaptable to change.

Career fields and occupations linked to combined results

Potential career fields are suggested (e.g. counselling or financial advising).

Some services provide an online link to these career fields, so you can explore them further.

The report will advise on the top occupations linked to your combined assessment.

This indicates typical work tasks as well as knowledge, skills and abilities required (e.g. radiology technician).

Other occupations to explore

From the range of occupation categories you may see alternative or wider career and job options. The report also suggests key options for jobs that link to your skills, interests and personality.

Career development: The report may provide a career development strategy.

It is about finding a good match for those starting a career or alternatives if there are few openings in a particular career area.

The assessment report can provide a guide to types of careers that may be fulfilling and interesting.

Specific careers

Other online career sites provide information on characteristics of different careers:

- Career areas (e.g. civil engineering).
- Assessment of the work type for a career (e.g. pharmacist).
- Knowledge requirements (e.g. for a social worker).
- Skill requirements (e.g. critical thinking or active listening).

- Abilities requirements (e.g. reasoning, comprehension or oral expression).
- Education requirements (degree and level).
- Wages and employment trends.

References

Career Assessment CPP: USA and Europe sites:

www.cpp.com (USA).

www.opp.com (Europe).

Grutter, J. and Hammer, L. *Strong and MBTI® Career Report*, CPP. Online career assessment example. www.cpp.com/en/strongproducts. aspx?pc=158 or via the short cut: https://tinyurl.com/ledvr3z

MBTI® Manual: A Guide to the Development and Use of the Myers-Briggs Type Indicator®. www.myersbriggs.org/my-mbti-personality-type/mbti-basics/ or via the short cut: https://tinyurl.com/2yhr4l

O*Net Online: Career database: www.Onetonline.com

Wikipedia. Myers-Briggs. https://en.wikipedia.org/wiki/Myers%E2%80%93Briggs_Type_Indicator or via the short cut: https://tinyurl.com/odcrvvn

Appendix Resources 3

General Achievement examples

This relates to Chapter 10: General Achievements and also to the corresponding Appendix Personal Plan: General Achievements.

Achievement statements

These are developed so they relate to various job selection criteria. Meeting a job's criteria is the basis used to select applicants for an interview and to select one applicant to secure the job.

Achievement statements are important in your job search preparation and in the job hunting process. They can form a framework for:

- Your resume (tailored to job application/criteria).
- Key points that you can recall when answering interview questions.

General Achievements: (covered in Chapter 10: General Achievements) include:

- Generic achievements.
- Other skills and achievements.
- Personal achievements.

These were developed as you completed your Personal Plan.
See Appendix Personal Plan 10: General Achievements.

Achievements Extended: (these covered in Chapter 11: Achievements – Extended):

- Profession-specific achievements.
- Job-specific achievements.

This book helps you develop your personal achievement statements.

It involves brainstorming your achievements or values; then developing one to three bullet points (or one to two lines) for each achievement topic.

Below are examples of achievement statements. Use them as a guide. You will develop your own achievement statements in two stages.

General achievements cover:

- Teamwork.
- Communication.
- People skills.
- Quality.
- Commitment.
- Timeliness.
- Customer service.

Teamwork achievement example

- My team work skills were initially developed during my employment at (company) during work experience. I recognise the value of building team skills.
- Teamwork skills have been important in my (role) at (company), which involved being part of a (e.g. accounting team). This required working with other team members and interacting with our clients.

Communication achievement example

- My written communication skills have developed during my university course via assignments and my thesis.

- My interpersonal and verbal skills are at a reasonably high level. I always seek to improve these. I recognise their importance for good work operations.

People skills achievement example

- My interpersonal skills are well developed; this will be important in interacting with a wide range of people within the organisation and possibly external clients.
- My personal characteristics include: easy to get on with and cooperative. These will assist in developing good relations with senior staff, other team members and managers.

Quality achievement example

- I take pride in completing quality work and projects. I have always sought to produce quality results in my university subjects (and part-time work).
- I have an understanding of the Quality Assurance standards for our profession for (e.g. road design).
- I have completed the Quality and Standards unit as part of my university course.

Commitment achievement example

- The completion of my university degree in (course) and completion of additional subjects (list any) have reflected a commitment in the way I operate.
- My part-time employment over the past four years at (company) has required both reliability and commitment. I have met and exceeded the requirements of my employer.

Timeliness achievement example

- I value timeliness. I seek to meet deadlines and be reliable in my time schedules involving others. I believe I have well developed attitudes to promptness and meeting agreed timeframes.

Customer service achievement example

- Client service skills have been developed in my part time work at (company), which involves my relating to and serving customers.

Other skills and achievements

These include:

- Word processing and spreadsheets.
- Computer and Internet.
- Software tools allied to your profession.

Word processing and spreadsheets

Many jobs involve tools such as word processing and spreadsheets, or the Internet. It is worthwhile outlining your achievements and skills.

For example:

- Word processing and spreadsheet skills – I have developed competence in using word processing software; I am adept at using spreadsheets.

Computer and Internet

Many jobs require general computing and Internet skills. It is worthwhile outlining your achievements and skills.

For example:

- Computer and Internet skills – I have a good level of proficiency using personal computers and the Internet.

Software tools

For many jobs, computer software tools may be a key part of the work. For example, if you are an architect or engineer then CAD (computer aided design) software is important. Identify your skills in any relevant software packages.

For example:

- CAD software – I have completed a course in (name) CAD system design.
- Applying CAD software ability – I have used CAD software for university projects and my skills are growing.

Personal achievements

Problem solving and analysis skills

These are important in many professions. Achievement statements reflect your ability or potential.
    For example:

- Problem solving and analysis – I have developed problem solving and analysis skills during my university course.
- I enjoy the challenge of solving problems and value my ability to critically analyse issues and develop solutions.

Self-motivation skills

Employers value this quality.
    For example:

- Self-motivation – I believe my self-motivation to get projects done would make me a valuable team member.
- Once I am given a task to undertake, I have the energy and motivation to complete it.

Appendix
Resources 4
Achievements
Extended examples

This relates to Chapter 11: Achievements Extended and to the corresponding Appendix Personal Plan 11: Achievements Extended.

Extended Achievement statements

These are developed so they relate to a selected profession and the various job selection criteria. The aim is to show you can meet the main job criteria.

Here we will provide examples of Extended Achievements:

- Profession-specific achievements.
- Job-specific achievements.
- Personal achievements.

Use them as a guide when you prepare your Personal Plan: Extended Achievements.

Profession-specific achievements

For each profession, there are specific requirements that are reflected in the job criteria. For example, if your career is in architecture, then visual presentation and graphics skills (computer aided design, CAD) are relevant.

For example:

- CAD software – I have completed a course in (name) CAD system design.
- Applying CAD software ability – I have used CAD software for university projects and my skills are growing.

Another example might be a pharmacist who will require skills that convert a customer's request to the most appropriate medication.

For example:

● Assessing customers needs – I believe it is important to develop skills to convert customers' needs to the most appropriate medication. I have sought to develop this skill in my practical training. I recognise its value and will develop this skill further.

Job-specific achievements

For different jobs, there can be some variations to the criteria. For example, if an engineering job requires workplace health and safety skills, your achievement statement may be:

● Workplace health and safety skills – I have completed a health and safety module for engineering sites. I recognise this is an important area in which to continue to develop.

Personal achievements

If you had a role as a secretary of a volunteer or sporting body, then this may be a valuable skill if it relates to the job you are seeking. It will reflect an ability to manage meetings, organisational demands and coordinate activities.

For example:

● Secretarial and coordination skills – In my role as secretary of (organisation), I have developed skills in managing meetings and coordinating the activities of other members of the organisation.

If you have done volunteer work in an aged care facility and your profession is in the healthcare area this may be relevant to the job you are seeking. You may want to highlight this achievement.

For example:

● Aged care skills – In my voluntary capacity, assisting at (organisation), I have developed an ability to relate to aged patients and assist them.

Appendix Resources 5

Foundation Resume example 1

This relates to Chapters 12 and 13: Preparing your Foundation Resume and to the corresponding Appendix Personal Plan 12 and 13: Foundation Resume stages 1 and 2.

Your Name

Address: **Home Phone**:   **Mobile**:   **Email**:

CAREER GOALS:

My aim is to move into a (type) career. I have completed a degree in (...).

I have evaluated my interests and completed a skills inventory that indicates this career direction would match my interests, skills and abilities. I can bring maturity, a good work ethic, teamwork and commitment to my employment.

OVERVIEW OF SKILLS & CAPABILITIES:

- Multi-skilled.
- Dependable.
- Physically fit.
- Degree in (. . .).

Key skills:

*Excellent interpersonal skills   *Good team member   *Self-motivated

*Work well independently   *Client focus

Personal characteristics:

*Friendly   *Strong work ethic   *Conscientious

*Trustworthy   *Positive attitude   *Sense of humour

GENERAL SKILLS:

Interpersonal skills:

- My interpersonal skills are well developed; this has been important in developing and maintaining good working relationships and friendships with senior staff, peers and clients.
- My personal characteristics, as previously stated, help build good relations.

Teamwork:

- Teamwork skills have been necessary in my various roles prior to undertaking my university course.
- Member of the quality assurance team at (company).
- Social Club team member at (group).
- Teamwork skills were initially developed during my employment at (...) during my university course.

Customer service:

- Client service skills have been developed in my role at (company), which involved providing customer services to clients.

Management and organisational skills:

- Disciplined worker with the ability to follow procedures precisely.
- Able to organise and prioritise tasks.

- Good time management skills allowing me to consistently meet deadlines.
- Patient, with the will to persevere in the face of obstacles.

Quality:

- I take pride in completing quality work in a timely, efficient manner.

PROFESSION-SPECIFIC SKILLS:

Accounting skills:

Accounting skills developed through my university course. Major in (topic).

Part-time work experience in processes surrounding (accounting function).

JOB-SPECIFIC SKILLS:

Computer skills:

Strong computer skills using Microsoft Excel, Word and various accounting packages. Good data entry skills. Ability to learn new software packages quickly.

Financial requirements:

Experience in preparing end of month accounts and sales reports for departmental manager.

Government compliance:

Good understanding from my university course (...) of government accounting requirements and reporting.

PERSONAL ACHIEVEMENTS:

Treasurer skills:

I have held the voluntary position of treasurer for (sporting organisation). This has provided me with knowledge and skills in accounting and finance related responsibilities.

KEY QUALIFICATIONS:

(Degree) majoring in (. . .).
University of . . .   year

Higher school certificate
(School)   year

EMPLOYMENT EXPERIENCE:

Role: (e.g. Accounting Assistant)
(Company)   month/year from – month/year to
(Company) specialises in (function)

Responsibilities: Preparation of monthly management accounts and financial reports, budgeting, reconciliations, maintain fixed asset register, government reporting and compliance, payroll and accounts payable functions.

Role (. . .)
(Company)   month/year from – month/year to

Responsibilities: Basic accounting duties from banking, end of month account preparation, statistical analysis and report preparation.

Role (e.g. Restaurant Employee (part-time) during university.)
(Organisation)   month/year from – month/year to

REFEREES AND REFERENCES:

- (name) (job title) (organisation) (phone) (email)
- (name) (job title) (organisation) (phone) (email)
- (name) (job title) (organisation) (phone) (email)

Appendix Resources 6

Foundation Resume example 2

This relates to Chapters 12 and 13: Preparing Your Foundation Resume –
stages 1 and 2, and to Appendices Personal Plan 12 and 13: Foundation
Resume – stages 1 and 2.

RESUME

Your Name

Address: **Home Phone:** ...   **Mobile:**   **Email:** ...

PERSONAL INFORMATION OVERVIEW:

University qualification

My degree in (...) through the University of (...) has provided me with a
wide range of skills that can be used in human resources and personnel
roles. These include specific courses in psychology and human resource
development.

Career goals

My career objectives involve employment in an organisation that can effectively use my human resource and people skills to contribute to business
operations. This may encompass administration duties, public relations and
client communications. My interests also include personal development
and marketing.

My aim is to build a positive professional career; and to provide positive contributions to my employer.

Profession skills overview

Through my educational qualifications, I have developed numerous business and work skills that relate to this role. These include effective administrative and organisational abilities. In my part-time roles during my course, I was able to develop further work skills. These include teamwork, customer relations and a focus on quality. My qualifications included subjects that cover human resources. Other areas where I feel I can contribute include marketing and human resource development.

General skills overview

These include well developed interpersonal skills and good team member skills. I am self-motivated and work well independently. I have a strong client focus.

Personal characteristics overview

These include a friendly personality, a sense of humour and a positive attitude. I have a strong work ethic. My past employers have commended me for being conscientious and trustworthy.

My personal profile reflects a strong interest in people, which is a key component of any organisation. I believe I have a strong empathy with people that is reflected in my good working relationships and teamwork skills. This has been coupled with a strong people focus in my undertakings that can be applied to business activities.

QUALIFICATIONS:

Year   Course (Organisation)

o Key areas of study: (. . .)

o Coaching on the job and goal setting.

Year   Course (Organisation)

o Key areas of study: (. . .)

o Training: planning and service delivery.

Year   Course (Organisation)

o Key areas of study: (. . .)

o Working within the retail environment.

o Occupation Health & Safety (OH&S).

o Customer relations.

Year – year   Bachelor of (. . .), University of (. . .)

- Developed skills and abilities in:
  - o Problem solving.
  - o Report writing.
  - o Computer skills.
  - o Teamwork.
- Key areas of study:
  - o Human Resources, psychology and marketing.

WORK EXPERIENCE:

---

year   Organisation: (. . .)   Role: Part-time (. . .)

o Duties: to conduct and assist the store manager with staff training.

year   Organisation: (. . .)   Role: Part-time Volunteer (. . .)

o Duties: Group Treasurer. To keep accurate financial records, monitor funds, acquit spending and prepare the annual budget.

year   Organisation: (. . .)   Role: Part-time Volunteer (. . .)

o Duties: President of my sporting association at university.

o Leadership, teamwork and coordination roles.

GENERAL WORK ABILITIES:

Administrative skills

o Effective organisation skills in my role as president of (name) residential college.

o Certificate IV in Assessment and Training.

Computer skills

o University level: Internet and email software training.

o University level: Microsoft Windows, Excel and Word.

Commercial skills

o Commercial training courses.

o Commercial employment via my part-time position at (organisation).

Customer service skills

o Well developed customer service standards through my part time role (organisation).

o Customer relations experience with (organisation).

Leadership skills

o In (year) I was president of (organisation). Its main function was responsibility for (activity). My duties involved leadership of the executive committee.

o Leadership role with (organisation). This involved running youth programmes through my local church. These involved planning and team organising.

Marketing skills

o Certificate II in Retail Operations.

o Marketing experience at (organisation).

Team skills

- ○ Teamwork and liaison skills through my role in (organisation) youth activities.

- ○ Team building and motivational leadership workshops and training. Conference (. . .).

INTERESTS AND ACTIVITIES:

- ○ (. . .)

- ○ (. . .)

REFEREES:

- ○ (name) (job title)   (organisation) (phone)   (email)

- ○ (name) (job title)   (organisation) (phone)   (email)

- ○ (name) (job title)   (organisation) (phone)   (email)

Appendix
Resources 7
Cover letter example 1

This relates to Chapter 16: Preparing your tailored cover letter.

Your cover letter may need changes to reflect region, country or contextual standard letter formats.

(date)

(Human Resources contact)

(Company address)

Dear (name or Sir/Madam, (but preferably by name))   Re: Position (. . .)

I noted with interest your recent advertisement for (position).

I have experience, enthusiasm and capabilities to successfully undertake this role.

My skills and qualifications include:

-
-

The position requires (select a couple of key criteria skills).

I can bring to this role and (company), experience and skills in this area. These include:

-
-

A key requirement is (select a couple of job requirements). My qualifications and past experience provide a sound base to undertake these responsibilities and contribute positively to (company's name) (function, e.g. customer service). These include:

-
-

My personal characteristics will relate to the position and its requirements. These include:

-
-

My experience, skills and work commitment would fit well with this position and its responsibilities. I would welcome the opportunity to work for (organisation).

I believe I can contribute positively in the planned role.

Please see my attached resume for further information to support this application.

I would welcome the opportunity for an interview to further discuss my application.

Yours faithfully, (if addressed to Dear Sir/Madam) or Yours sincerely, (if addressed to actual name)

(Name)   (email)   (address)   (telephone number)

Appendix
Resources 8

Cover letter example 2

This relates to Chapter 16: Preparing your tailored cover letter.

Your cover letter may need changes to reflect region, country or contextual standard letter formats.

(date)

(Human Resources contact)

(Company address)

Dear (name or Sir/Madam, (but preferably by name))   Re: Position (. . .)

I noted with interest your recent advertisement for (position).

I have experience, enthusiasm and capabilities to successfully undertake this role.

My skills and qualifications and include:

- (degree).
- (other relevant educational qualifications).
- (other skills related to job criteria).
- (other general skills related to job . . . , e.g. Word, Excel, etc.).

A key requirement * is (...skills). My qualifications and past experience provide a sound base to undertake these responsibilities and contribute positively to (company) and its (function, e.g. customer service).

The position ** requires (...skills, e.g. teamwork and good interpersonal skills). I can bring to this role and (company) skills in this area.

The experience, skills and work commitment I can offer would fit well with this position and its responsibilities. Please see my attached resume for further information to support this application.

I would welcome the opportunity for an interview to further discuss the opportunity to work for you and contribute to (company).

Yours faithfully, (if addressed to Dear Sir/Madam) or Yours sincerely, (if addressed to actual name)

(Name)

(email)   (address)   (telephone number)

*Note: Pick out two or three main job criteria requirements or job criteria and address them in two to three lines in total or a short statement.

**Note: Pick out two or three other main position requirements and address them in two to three lines in total or a short statement.

Appendix Resources 9
Interviews – experts' advice

This relates to Chapters 10 and 17.

The following provides a short review of Firestone's (2014) *Ultimate Guide to Job Interview – Answers*. It is a valuable and informative book.

It has been included in the Appendix Resources as an addendum for Chapter 17: Interviews.

The fundamental interview questions

Understand the Three Fundamental Bases for Questions

All interview questions are a variation of three fundamental questions:

- "Can you do the job?
- Will you reasonably like the job and stay motivated?
- Will we like working with you?" (Firestone, 2014: p. 6)

Interview

"A lot is determined in the first 30 seconds of an interview" (Firestone, 2014: p. 8).

Consider tone, outward appearance, how others gauge your personality and professionalism from the first impression. Practice "your entrance, smile, handshake, demeanour, gravitas and first words" (Firestone, 2014: p. 8).

The First Impression and Entrance is Important

Evaluation

Many questions will focus on the job criteria: can you do the job?

- Others on: will you like the job and stay?
  - o Will you fit with the corporate culture?
  - o They will check you against these factors (BRAVE): Behave/Relate/Attitude/Values/Environment
- Others on: will we like working with you?
  - o Use the tips and strategies to increase your "likeability".

Analyse the job description: what are they really looking for?

Job Criteria – What are they Looking For?

Preparing for your interview

The book explains:

- Competency-based interviews: they look for examples to show your abilities or competencies.
- The job seeker should prepare for the interview in order to be able to talk about achievements and link them to the job role.
- Behavioural questions ask you to "describe a challenge, problem or situation from the past and explain the outcome or result" (Firestone, 2014: p. 19).
- This is followed by questions to probe your "mindset, attitudes and thought processes" (Firestone, 2014: p. 19).
- Example question: "Describe a situation when …" (Firestone, 2014: p. 19).

- Follow-up probe question: "What steps did you take?" (Firestone, 2014: p. 20).

- Basic answer format: Yes, to answer your question, we had a situation where the problem was . . . . The action I took was . . . . Due to my efforts and competencies a positive outcome was . . . .

- Quote back in your answers specific metrics on what you achieved, for example, I helped increase customer service satisfaction by 20%.

Understand the Behavioural Interview Approach

SOARL

After reading Firestone's (2014) book, you should be able to identify and write out four to eight SOARL stories:

- Situation: what was the problem?
- Objective: what did you need to achieve?
- Action: what did you do?
- Results: what was the outcome?
- Learning approach: what did you learn?

Example SOARL question

Please give us an example of how you solved a customer service issue in your part time job.

Example SOARL answer

Yes, let me give you an example of . . .

The objective was to . . .

The action I took was . . .

The outcome results were positive and the outcome was . . .

I learnt that . . . .

Creating SOARL stories

- Brainstorm examples.
- Write out short responses for each SOARL key point.
- Edit them so they are short, easily presented and have an impact.

Develop and Write Down Your Competencies (Achievements)

Develop and write down your competencies (achievements)

Main behavioural competencies

Firestone (2014) identifies:

- Competency is the ability to get something done. Firestone identifies 40 competencies.
- Some main ones that relate to graduate positions include: analytical thinking and problem solving; applying technology to tasks; continual learning; customer service; flexibility; initiative; integrity; interpersonal skills; communication; planning and priority management; relationships; resilience; risk management; results orientation; teamwork; and technical skills.
- Recognise that interviews are about an investigation into your behavioural competencies.
- You can then focus on the main information you need to convey. It is about "selling yourself" and impressing the interviewers.

40 core "behavioural competencies"

Firestone (2014) identifies these competencies (these are similar to achievements). He groups them into common themes:

- Managing yourself: analytical thinking and problem solving; applying technology to tasks; continual learning; customer service; flexibility;

initiative; integrity; interpersonal skills; communication; relationships; resilience; and teamwork.

- Managing projects: decision making; planning and priority management; relationships; and technical skills.
- Leading and managing people: empowering others; change management; and teamwork.
- Leading and managing programmes: creative thinking; management; and risk management.
- Leading and managing organisations: strategic thinking and vision.

Interview questions and answers

Firestone (2014: pp. 56–112) provides a wide range of questions and advice on how to respond to them. The questions include:

- "Tell me a little bit about yourself..."

  "Prepare and practice an opening statement...keep it under 90 seconds."

  Personal introduction (10 seconds)...In terms of career (30 seconds).

  What excites me about this job (or company) (30 seconds).

  Wrap it up: (how can I help you in terms of this job?).
- "Why do you want to work here?"
- "Why should we hire you?"
- "In what ways do you think you can make a contribution to our company?"
- "What do you consider to be your greatest strengths and weaknesses?"
- "What have you learnt from your mistakes?"
- "Give me an example of a problem you faced... and tell me how you solved it."
- "Describe a situation when working with a team produced more successful results than if you had completed the project on your own."
- "Are you good at delegating tasks? Tell me about your process."

- "Describe the most creative thing you have ever done."

- "What motivates you to go the extra mile on a project or job?"

- "Give me an example of a time you did more than what was required in your job."

- "What steps do you follow to study a problem before making a decision?"

- "Do you have any hobbies? What do you do in your spare time? What would you like me to know about you that is not on your resume?"

- "You may be overqualified (or too experienced) for the position we have to offer."

Prepare Your Responses to Interview Questions

Yes and no questions

- Do not just reply "yes" or "no". Add in extra information to "sell yourself".

- Give a quick example with a positive outcome.

- Question: "Can you use ABC software?"

- Answer: "Yes I was trained on it and I developed some new techniques, etc."

Interview "do's and don'ts"

Advice from Firestone (2014) includes:

- Do not take your accomplishments for granted.

- Make them measurable.

- Do not overdo it and give too many examples.

- Do not be overly talkative.

- Do not criticise others.

- Do not enquire about salary or conditions until you get an offer.

- Do not feel pressured to answer every question. "I have not done that" is acceptable.

Questions you can ask

- What type of person are you looking for and how does the position fit into the overall organisation?
- "Are there areas where an extra effort could really make a difference?" (Firestone, 2014: p. 122).

Closing statement

Firestone (2014) advises:

- Have a power statement to close the interview.
- A short concluding statement (less than 60 seconds).
- Market yourself as a good candidate for the position.
- Add a statement of interest and enthusiasm to work for the manager (or organisation).

Practice a Power Statement to Close Off the Interview

Reference

Firestone, B. (2014). *Ultimate Guide to Job Interview – Answers*. (Success Patterns, Santa Monica, CA, 7th edn).

Appendix Resources 10

Targeted Resume – Australian example

This appendix relates to Chapter 15 (this is an indicative example).

Your Name

Address: **Home Phone**:   **Mobile**:   **Email**:

CAREER GOALS:

My aim is to move into a (type) career. I have completed a degree in (. . .).

I have evaluated my interests and completed a skills inventory that indicates this career direction would match my interests, skills and abilities. I can bring maturity, a good work ethic, teamwork and commitment to my employment.

EDUCATION AND TRAINING:

(Degree) majoring in (. . .).
University of . . .   year

Higher School Certificate
(School)   year

SKILLS AND CAPABILITIES:

- Multi-skilled.
- Dependable.
- Physically fit.

Key skills:

Excellent interpersonal skills   Good team member   Self-motivated

Work well independently   Client focus

Personal characteristics:

Friendly   Strong work ethic   Conscientious

Trustworthy   Positive attitude   Sense of humour

GENERAL SKILLS:

Interpersonal skills:

- My interpersonal skills are well developed; this has been important in developing and maintaining good working relationships and friendships with senior staff, peers and clients.
- My personal characteristics, as previously stated, help build good relations.

Teamwork:

- Teamwork skills have been necessary in my various roles prior to undertaking my university course.
- Member of the quality assurance team at (company).
- Social Club team member at (group).
- Teamwork skills were initially developed during my employment at (...) during my university course.

Customer service:

- Client service skills have been developed in my role at (company).

Management and organisational skills:

- Disciplined worker with the ability to follow procedures precisely.
- Able to organise and prioritise tasks.
- Good time management skills allowing me to consistently meet deadlines.

Quality:

- I take pride in completing quality work in a timely, efficient manner.

PROFESSION-SPECIFIC SKILLS

Accounting skills:

Accounting skills developed through my university course. Major in (topic).

Part-time work experience in processes surrounding (accounting function).

JOB-SPECIFIC SKILLS:

Computer skills:

Strong computer skills using Microsoft Excel, Word and various accounting packages. Good data entry skills. Ability to learn new software packages quickly.

Financial requirements:

Experience in preparing end of month accounts and sales reports for departmental manager.

Government compliance:

Good understanding from my university course (...) of government accounting requirements and reporting.

PERSONAL ACHIEVEMENTS:

Treasurer skills:

- I have held the voluntary position of treasurer for (sporting organisation). This has provided me with knowledge and skills in accounting and finance related responsibilities.

AWARDS AND ACHIEVEMENTS:

(Include any relevant awards).

EMPLOYMENT EXPERIENCE:

Role: (e.g. Accounting Assistant)
(Company)   month/year from – month/year to
(Company specialises in (function)

Responsibilities: Preparation of monthly management accounts and financial reports, budgeting, reconciliations, maintain fixed asset register, government reporting and compliance, payroll and accounts payable functions.

Role: (...)
(Company)   month/year from   – month/year to

Responsibilities: Basic accounting duties from banking, end of month account preparation, statistical analysis and report preparation

Role: (e.g. Restaurant Employee (part-time) during university.)
(Organisation)   month/year from – month/year to

REFEREES AND REFERENCES:

- (name) (job title)   (organisation) (phone)   (email)
- (name) (job title)   (organisation) (phone)   (email)
- (name) (job title)   (organisation) (phone)   (email)

Appendix Resources 11

Targeted Resume – United Kingdom (UK) example

Relates to Chapter 15 (this is an indicative example)

Your Name

Address: **Home Phone**:   **Mobile**:   **Email**:

PERSONAL STATEMENT:

My aim is to move into a (type) career. I have completed a degree in (. . .).

I have evaluated my interests and completed a skills inventory that indicates this career direction would match my interests, skills and abilities. I can bring maturity, a good work ethic, teamwork and commitment to my employment.

EDUCATION AND TRAINING:

(Degree) majoring in (. . .)

University of . . .   year

Modules completed: (. . .)

School (name)   years

A Levels: (. . .)

GCSE: (subjects (results))

EMPLOYMENT EXPERIENCE:

Role: (e.g. Accounting Assistant)
(Company)   month/year from – month/year to
(Company) specialises in (function)

Responsibilities: Preparation of monthly management accounts and financial reports, budgeting, reconciliations, maintain fixed asset register, government reporting and compliance, payroll and accounts payable functions.

Role: (. . .)
(Company)   month/year from – month/year to

Responsibilities: Basic accounting duties from banking, end of month account preparation, statistical analysis and report preparation.

Role: (e.g. Restaurant Employee (part-time) during university.)
(Organisation)   month/year from – month/year to

PROFESSION-SPECIFIC SKILLS: Accounting skills:

Accounting skills developed through my university course. Major in (topic).

Part-time work experience in processes surrounding (accounting function).

JOB-SPECIFIC SKILLS:

Computer skills:

Strong computer skills using Microsoft Excel, Word and various accounting packages.

Good data entry skills. Ability to learn new software packages quickly.

Financial requirements:

Experience in preparing end of month accounts and sales reports for departmental manager.

Government compliance:

Good understanding from my university course (. . .) of government accounting requirements and reporting.

Teamwork:

- Teamwork skills have been necessary in my various roles prior to undertaking my university course.
- Member of the quality assurance team at (company).
- Social Club team member at (group).

Teamwork skills were initially developed during my employment at (. . .) during my university course.

Customer service:

- Client service skills have been developed in my role at (company).

Management and organisational skills:

- Disciplined worker with the ability to follow procedures precisely.
- Able to organise and prioritise tasks.
- Good time management skills allowing me to consistently meet deadlines.

Quality:

- I take pride in completing quality work in a timely, efficient manner.

PERSONAL SKILLS AND CAPABILITIES:

Key skills:

Excellent interpersonal skills   Good team member   Self-motivated

Work well independently   Client focus

Personal characteristics:

Friendly   Strong work ethic   Conscientious

Trustworthy   Positive attitude   Sense of humour

Interpersonal skills:

My interpersonal skills are well developed; this has been important in developing and maintaining good working relationships and friendships with senior staff, peers and clients.

PERSONAL ACHIEVEMENTS:

Treasurer skills:

I have held the voluntary position of Treasurer for (sporting organisation). This has provided me with knowledge and skills in accounting and finance related responsibilities.

AWARDS AND ACHIEVEMENTS:

(Include any relevant awards).

REFEREES AND REFERENCES:

- (name) (job title)   (organisation) (phone)   (email)
- (name) (job title)   (organisation) (phone)   (email)
- (name) (job title)   (organisation) (phone)   (email)

Appendix Resources 12

Targeted Resume – USA example

This appendix relates to Chapter 15: Preparing your Targeted Resume: country-specific. There is no standard layout, but it may include the following:

Name: Address: Contacts: email/phone

CAREER STATEMENT

EDUCATION

University: Degree course:

Completed date: GPA (grade point average):

College: name and location

Completed courses in:

High school: name and location

SELECTED COURSEWORK or ACADEMIC PROJECTS

● Main modules.

AWARDS

WORK EXPERIENCE

- Company, location:
- Position: Dates: from   to
- Role or achievements:

(Repeat for others in reverse chronological order.)

SKILLS

- Organisation: Location: Dates:
- Role or position:
- Skills:

(Repeat for others in reverse chronological order.)

ACTIVITIES

VOLUNTEER EXPERIENCE or COMMUNITY SERVICE

- Organisation: Role: Years:

CERTIFICATES

REFERENCES

Appendix Resources 13

Targeted Resume – European example

This appendix relates to Chapter 15: Preparing your Targeted Resume: country-specific.

The Europass CV is the backbone of the Europass Portfolio of documents. It provides an online wizard and templates to ensure consistency of headings.

See Europass CV examples and Europass templates in the References at the end of this appendix.

The main contents are:

Personal information:

Name, address, phone, email, website.

Type of application:

Job applied for, position, personal statement.

Work experience:

Date from; date to; position; employer (name, city, country); main responsibilities.

Education and training:

Date from; date to; qualification; organisation (city, country); organisation European Qualifications Framework (EQF) or national classification.

Personal skills:

- Mother tongue.

- Other languages (capability: listening, reading, spoken, writing); diploma or certificate.

- Communication skills.

- Organisational or managerial skills.

- Job-related skills.

- Digital competence
  - Information processing.
  - Communication.
  - Content creation.
  - Safety.
  - Problem solving.
  - Other computer skills.
  - Certificates (for any of the above).

Additional competences:

Emphasising technical, organisational, artistic and social skills.

Optional information:

Details that might be added to the Europass CV in the form of annexes.

References

Europass CV. Examples are available in multiple languages: http://europass.cedefop.europa.eu/documents/curriculum-vitae/examples

Europass Templates. The templates are available in multiple EU languages: http://europass.cedefop.europa.eu/documents/curriculum-vitae/templates-instructions

Appendix Resources 14

Targeted Resume – Asian example

This appendix relates to Chapter 15: Preparing your Targeted Resume: country-specific.

There is no standard layout. Size is usually two to three pages. Content and order can vary. Typical layout can include the following:

Name:

Personal contact details: phone; email; nationality.

Career objective: Describe your career goals and position sought in a concise paragraph.

or

Executive summary: Overview of your resume in concise form. Key points.

or

Personal profile: Short summary paragraph.

Education:

University degree	University years
Key modules completed	and results
High school education	School years

Special and technical skills:

Language skills:

-

Computer skills:

-

Key skills: Include concise information under main relevant headings such as team work, leadership, etc.

-

Work experience/professional experience:

Company   years (from/to)

- Role; skills developed and achievements.

Volunteer or community service experience:

Personal interests:

- Sports activities.
- Other interests.

Personal information:

Sex   Marital status   Date of birth

Permanent address   Nationality   ID number (if applicable or required)

Military experience: If applicable or required.

Professional membership:

References:

In some cases, list name, organisation and contact information, or "available on request".

Appendix
Personal Plan 1 – aims

This relates to Chapter 1: Getting prepared.
My priority goals:
My short term actions:

What are the three priority goals I need to focus on now?

-
-
-

What are your main short-term actions to reach these goals? (What are you going to do?)

-
-
-

Personal Plan

My commitment:
Completing a Personal Plan:

- Consider the benefits of completing the Personal Plan as you work through the book.

- Consider the risks and drawbacks of not doing the Personal Plan as you work through the book. Thinking you will do it later often does not happen owing to other personal demands.

- I undertake to complete the Personal Plan to help me succeed in my transition from university to a career:

Name: ....

Date: ....

Appendix

Personal Plan 2 – challenges and issues

This relates to Chapter 1: Getting prepared, and covers my priority challenges and my priority actions.

What are the three priority challenges to work on further?

-
-
-

What am I going to do about these challenges? My priority actions are:

-
-
-

Appendix

Personal Plan 3 – one step at a time

This relates to Chapter 1: Getting prepared.

Identify a large project or activity that you face as you prepare for employment.

Break it down into smaller tasks, which you can do.

Individual exercise: identify larger project or activity

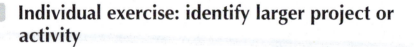

What is a larger project or activity you would like to do as you prepare for employment?

....

Individual exercise: break it down

Personal brainstorm: now break it into smaller tasks to do. List these tasks to achieve the desired project or activity goal:

....

....

....

....

....

....

....

Appendix

Personal Plan 4 – job selection psychology

This relates to Chapter 4: Job hunting – key factors and the section 4.4 Job selection psychology.

There is a deeper psychological reason why a manager or supervisor employs a person. It is based on the key question: will the potential employee help the manager to:

- do his or her work better;
- support the manager's goals (these may be personal goals or performance targets);
- make the organisation or business successful; and
- overcome problems and challenges the manager is facing.

How can you respond to these deeper psychological motivations? It can be done easily by preparing, writing and practising short statements that respond to these needs. These short "helping statements" can be selectively added onto your interview responses.

In response to a question about your qualifications, you can reply by just listing them. Alternatively, you can list them in your response and add a "helping statement" at the end. For example: "my qualifications are (...), which I believe can contribute to your goals."

Focus on developing "helping statements". These relate to assisting the manager (outlined in bullet points above); for example, "which can contribute to your work programme".

Now prepare four added "helping statements":

-
-
-
-

Learn and practise these. They can be useful in both the job application stage, but more so in the interview stage. They seek to connect your abilities and skills, via your response, to the deeper needs of the manager; that is, to have staff who can help the manager to do his or her job better and more successfully.

Appendix
Personal Plan 5 – locating jobs

This relates to Chapter 5: Locating job opportunities.
Should you seek professional advice to help locate jobs?

Of the different job market sectors or organisations, which types of organisations offer the best potential for helping you to locate job opportunities?

-
-
-
-

What job search agency will you approach or use?
(This may require an Internet search or advice):

-
-
-
-

What actions do you intend to take?

-
-
-

Social media (for job hunting): LinkedIn, Facebook, Google Plus and Twitter:

Note: This part of your Personal Plan is a preliminary review of the social media as an option.

It will be covered in detail later in:

- Chapter 6: Social media for job search: options.
- Chapter 7: Social media: establishing your online profile.
- Chapter 8: Social media for job hunting.

What are your initial feelings about using social media for job searching?

-
-

Are there any barriers for you to use social media for job searching?

-
-

What are the positive opportunities for you to use social media for job searching?

-
-
-

What are your preliminary plans to use social media for job searching?

-
-

Appendix

Personal Plan 6 – social media online profile

This relates to Chapter 7: Social media – establishing your online profile.

LinkedIn profile

Let us use LinkedIn to build your professional online profile (bio or biography).

Approach

This is a preliminary version. You can come back later after you have completed your Foundation Resume to update and improve your online bio.

Create a professional LinkedIn profile link

Your url name/address. LinkedIn will advise on options:

. . . .

Select a professional profile photo

Crop and edit it; then upload it.

. . . .

Add a "summary" to your profile

This should include a few short paragraphs, summarising your professional strengths, experience, skills and training. It should be easy for employers to scan read quickly:

-
-
-

Industry selection

At the top of your profile, next to your photo and name, you can create a headline and choose an industry. These are important, because these are how companies search for individuals. Provide an accurate job title and choose an industry, and you will be much easier to find.

Check other profiles and keywords for your chosen career/industry.

-
-
-

Experience section

This is a preliminary version. You can come back later after you have completed your Foundation Resume to update and improve your online bio. (Copy and paste the appropriate information from your resume to the website.)

Include your employment work experience as well as any volunteer work experience.

-
-
-

Additional information in your profile

Show any links to Facebook, Twitter accounts or information that you think prospective employers would like to see. Include any personal attributes from your resume that relate to the job you are seeking.

-
-
-

Appendix
Personal Plan 7 – SWOT analysis

This relates to Chapter 9: Personal development.

Decision-making tools: SWOT analysis

SWOT is short for Strengths, Weaknesses, Opportunities and Threats. It is a practical approach to address issues. Under four headings you assess the situation:

- Your strengths.
- Your weaknesses.
- Your opportunities.
- Your threats.

For each one, just write down bullet points or short phrases that relate to you and the situation.

By brainstorming these headings, you are addressing an issue in a systematic way. You are looking at both the positives and negatives. The positives – the strengths and opportunities –will help you identify your advantages. The negatives – weaknesses and threats – help you see issues that may need attention.

The issue

Use a short, one-line statement on the topic you are seeking to understand or resolve.

It is worthwhile spending some time on this. By getting the issue clear in your mind and identified, it helps as you to move forward. The key question is, is this the main issue or a minor aspect?

-
-

Strengths

Brainstorm your strengths in relation to the issue. Write these down as bullet points or short phrases. Questions you could be asking yourself include:

- What are you good at naturally?
- What skills have you worked to develop?
- What are your talents, or natural-born gifts?
- Do you have a large network on social media?
- What do your teachers and fellow students see as your strengths?
- What values and ethics set you apart from your peers?

-
-
-
-

Weaknesses

Brainstorm your weaknesses in relation to the issue. Write these down as bullet points or short phrases, by answering the following questions:

- What are your negative work habits and traits?
- What parts of your education or training need improving?
- What would other people see as your weaknesses?

- Where/how can you improve yourself?
- What are you afraid to do or most likely to avoid?
- What negative feedback about your personality or work habits have you received from your teachers, friends or family?

-
-
-
-
-

Opportunities

Brainstorm your opportunities in relation to the issue. Write these down as bullet points or short phrases. Again, ask yourself some questions:

- How is the state of the economy in your sector or your region?
- Is your industry a growth industry or not?
- What are the new technologies in your industry?
- Is there a new demand for a skill or trait that you possess?
- What are the biggest changes happening in the current employment environment?
- Have teachers or fellow students given you feedback about new services that you could provide or ways to improve your manner?

-
-
-
-

Threats

Brainstorm your threats (or barriers) in relation to the issue. Write these down as bullet points or short phrases. By asking these questions, you force yourself towards honest responses.

- Is your selected career contracting or changing direction?
- What is the competition for the types of jobs for which you are best suited?
- Do your weaknesses inhibit your ability to get a promotion in your company or to change jobs?
- What are the largest external dangers to your career objectives?
- Are there any new professional standards you cannot meet?
- Are there any new educational qualifications or certification requirements that will impede your progress?

-
-
-
-

Application

Review your responses above. You have set out both the positives and negatives. These will help you see an issue more clearly and help in your decision making.

It will help you build on your strengths and address any areas that you may feel are barriers or weaknesses. The process will assist you as you make career and job decisions.

Appendix
Personal Plan 8 – decision balance analysis

This relates to Chapter 9: Personal development.

Decision-making tools: decision balance analysis

Compare this technique to that of the SWOT analysis explained in Appendix Personal Plan 7.

You may want to use some of the same questions.

Present situation (short sentence or bullet points):

-
-
-

Desired outcome (short sentence or bullet points):

-
-
-

Possible or proposed options (short sentence or bullet points):

-
-
-

The decision balance analysis

Assessing the proposed option: what will happen if I choose this course of action?

Myself (bullet points for your response):

Gains for self:	Acceptable to me because:	Not acceptable to me because:
Losses for self:	Acceptable to me because:	Not acceptable to me because:

Significant others if applicable (bullet points as your response):

Gains for significant other:	Acceptable to me because:	Not acceptable to me because:
Losses for significant other:	Acceptable to me because:	Not acceptable to me because:

Work colleagues (if applicable) (bullet points as your response):

Gains for work setting:	Acceptable to me because:	Not acceptable to me because:
Losses for work setting:	Acceptable to me because:	Not acceptable to me because:

Appendix

Personal Plan 9 – force field analysis

This relates to Chapter 9: Personal development.

Decision-making tools: force field analysis

Present situation:

Desired outcome:

Forces that help me to reach the desired outcome:	Actions to maximise these forces:
•	• . . . .
•	• . . . .
•	• . . . .
•	• . . . .
•	• . . . .

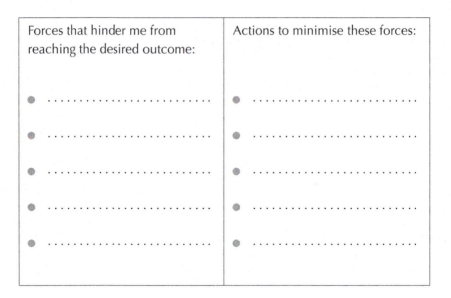

Forces that hinder me from reaching the desired outcome:	Actions to minimise these forces:
•	• . . . .
•	• . . . .
•	• . . . .
•	• . . . .
•	• . . . .

 ## Action plan

From your maximising and minimising list, identify your proposed actions:

Action   **Priority**

(1 = 1st, 2 = 2nd)

• . . . .

• . . . .

• . . . .

• . . . .

• . . . .

• . . . .

• . . . .

I will do the following:
(Set a timeframe that is not too tight, but also not too distant, perhaps a week or fortnight.)

Target date . . . . . .

Action: . . . .
. . . .
. . . .
. . . .

Target date . . . . . .

Action: . . . .
. . . .
. . . .
. . . .

Target date . . . . . .

Action: . . . .
. . . .
. . . .
. . . .

Appendix

Personal Plan 10 – general achievements

This relates to Chapter 10: General achievements.

See also Appendix Resources 3: General achievement statements examples.

These examples will help you complete your achievement statements below.

Approach

- You will brainstorm your achievements with a heading for each topic.

- Refine these into short statements and edit them so they are well expressed.

- For each achievement you will come up with two or three short achievement statements; they will be one to three lines to keep it brief. If you cannot think of actual examples, then add in your value statement.

Examples are given in the Appendix Resources 3: General achievement statements.

Generic achievements

Teamwork

Brainstorm achievements for this topic (just a heading to identify it).

-

-

-

Write an achievement statement for each one.

-

-

-

Communication

Brainstorm achievements for this topic (just a heading to identify it).

-

-

-

Write an achievement statement for each one.

-

-

-

People skills

Brainstorm achievements for this topic (just a heading to identify it).

-
-
-

Write an achievement statement for each one.

-
-
-

Quality

Brainstorm achievements for this topic (just a heading to identify it).

-
-
-

Write an achievement statement for each one.

-

-

-

Commitment

Brainstorm achievements for this topic (just a heading to identify it).

-

-

-

Write an achievement statement for each one.

-

-

-

Timeliness

Brainstorm achievements for this topic (just a heading to identify it).

-

-

-

Write an achievement statement for each one.

-

-

-

Customer service

Brainstorm achievements for this topic (just a heading to identify it).

-

-

-

Write an achievement statement for each one.

●

●

●

These will be the basis for your Foundation Resume for the general criteria. This will follow shortly.

Other skills and achievements

These include general skills such as word processing, spreadsheets, computer and Internet use.

Now complete your Personal Plan for these.

Word processing and spreadsheets

Brainstorm achievements for this topic (just a heading to identify it).

●

●

●

Write an achievement statement for each one.

-

-

-

Computer and Internet

Brainstorm achievements for this topic (just a heading to identify it).

-

-

-

Write an achievement statement for each one.

-

-

-

Software tools

For many jobs, computer software tools may be a key part of the work. Identify any computer tools that are essential or widely used in your profession.

Brainstorm achievements for this topic (just a heading to identify it).

●

●

●

Write an achievement statement for each one.

●

●

●

Personal achievements

Other skills and achievement criteria include problem solving and analysis, and self-motivation.

Problem solving and analysis skills

Brainstorm achievements for this topic (just a heading to identify it).

●

●

●

Write an achievement statement for each one.

-

-

-

Self-motivation skills

Brainstorm achievements for this topic (just a heading to identify it).

-

-

-

Write an achievement statement for each one.

-

-

-

Appendix
Personal Plan 11 – Achievements Extended

This relates to Chapter 11: Achievements Extended – further selling points.

See also Appendix Resources 4: Achievements Extended examples.

These examples will help you complete your achievement statements below.

Approach

- You will brainstorm your achievements with a heading for each topic.

- Refine these into succinct and short statements and edit them so they are well expressed.

- For each achievement you will come up with two or three short achievement statements; they will be one to three lines to keep it brief. If you cannot think of actual examples, then add in your value statement.

Examples are given in Appendix Resources 4: Achievements Extended examples.

There are three achievement phases below, which you should complete progressively. Just complete each one as guided by the Personal Plan steps in Chapter 11: Achievements Extended.

Profession-specific achievements

These will come from the job criteria.

First, identify them:

List the main professional criteria (just a heading or short sentence to identify it).

-

-

-

-

-

Write an achievement statement for each one; just a one- or two-line short
statement).

-

-

-

-

-

-

Job-specific achievements

These are listed in the criteria for a particular job. You will need to prepare your short achievement statements. This can be done for each job application if there are new aspects that are not already covered in your preparation.

First, identify them:

List the main job-specific criteria (just a heading or short sentence to identify it).

●

●

●

●

Write an achievement statement for each one.

●

●

●

●

●

Personal achievements

These may be added skills or achievements from other activities you have done. Perhaps a role in a sporting organisation, volunteer activities, part-time roles or other awards.

We are looking for personal achievements that relate to a job or career area.

First, identify them:

List the personal achievements that relate to the job or job criteria (just a heading or short sentence to identify it).

-
-
-

Write an achievement statement for each one.

-
-
-

Appendix

Personal Plan 12 –
Foundation Resume
stage 1 key points

This relates to Chapter 12: Preparing your Foundation Resume – Stage 1.

Approach

- You will prepare short paragraphs that correspond to the main resume headings. These will be key parts of your Foundation Resume.

- You have already completed your Personal Plan: General Achievements (if not, this is a necessary stage for you to complete now).

- You will convert the short achievement statements you have developed into short resume statements for the relevant parts below.

Examples of Foundation Resumes:

- Appendix Resources 5: Foundation Resume example 1.
- Appendix Resources 6: Foundation Resume example 2.

You will draw on your Personal Plan 10: General Achievements.

Career goals

A short paragraph or several short one-line statements that show your career goals in relation to this job.

-

-

-

Overview of skills and abilities

Bullet points summary of your main skills and capabilities, related to the type of job.

-

-

-

-

Key skills

A summary: selection of a few bullet points that relate you to the key skills required for the job.

-

-

-

Personal characteristics

Short sentence or bullet points where these can show your personal characteristics.

-
-
-

Interests and activities

Short sentence or bullet points where these can show your wider activities and abilities.

-
-
-

General skills

Here you can draw on your Personal Plan 10: General Achievements that you have already completed. Other examples are given in the Appendix Resources 3: General Achievements examples.

The list below covers a wide range of jobs and some of the more common general job criteria.

You will need to assess for your potential job and career plans and decide which of these are relevant.

You will just include those that relate to your main career option at this stage.

Teamwork

Write a resume statement for this topic from your Personal Plan: General Achievements.

•

•

Communication

Write a resume statement for this topic from your Personal Plan: General Achievements.

•

•

People skills

Write a resume statement for this topic from your Personal Plan: General Achievements.

•

•

Quality

Write a resume statement for this topic from your Personal Plan: General Achievements.

-
-

Commitment

Write a resume statement for this topic from your Personal Plan: General Achievements.

-
-

Timeliness

Write a resume statement for this topic from your Personal Plan: General Achievements.

-
-

Customer service

Write a resume statement for this topic from your Personal Plan: General Achievements.

-
-

These are the inputs for your Foundation Resume. They are common criteria for many jobs.

Focus on those that are relevant to your profession and career.

Other skills and achievements

These include skills such as word processing, spreadsheets, computer and Internet use.

Now complete your Personal Plan: Foundation Resume for these.

Word processing and spreadsheets

Write a resume statement for this topic from your Personal Plan: General Achievements.

●

●

Computer and Internet

Write a resume statement for this topic from your Personal Plan: General Achievements.

●

●

Software tools

For many jobs, computer software tools may be a key part of the work. Identify any computer tools that are essential or widely used in your profession.

Write a resume statement for this topic from your Personal Plan: General Achievements.

●

●

Personal achievements

Other skills and achievement criteria include problem solving and analysis, and self-motivation.

Problem solving and analysis skills

Write a resume statement for this topic from your Personal Plan: General Achievements.

●

●

Self-motivation skills

Write a resume statement for this topic from your Personal Plan: General Achievements.

●

●

Key qualifications

Short one-line statement:

University qualifications:

    o

Other qualifications:

    o

    o

Other courses and achievements:

    o

    o

    o

Employment experience

This can be specific employment-related experience as well as more general work experience.

Work experience (year and organisation).

    o

    o

    o

Work experience (year and organisation).

    o

    o

    o

Appendix

Personal Plan 13 – Foundation Resume stage 2

This relates to Chapter 13: Preparing your Foundation Resume – stage 2. Examples of Foundation Resumes are given in:

- Appendix Resources 5: Foundation Resume example 1.
- Appendix Resources 6: Foundation Resume example 2.

You will draw on your Personal Plan 11: Achievements Extended for inputs to this part of your plan.

This part of your Personal Plan relates to specific profession and job criteria. You will convert your Achievements Extended statements into your Foundation Resume.

Approach

- You have already completed your Personal Plan: Achievements Extended (if not, this is a necessary stage for you to complete now).
- You will convert the short achievement statements you have developed into short resume statements.
- Refine these into short statements; edit them so they are well expressed.
- For each achievement, you will come up with one to three short statements for the resume topic. (It should be just one to three lines to keep it brief. If you cannot think of actual examples then add in your value statement.)

Foundation Resume: profession-specific

For each profession there are specific selection criteria to be met.

These profession-specific criteria have already been identified in Chapter 11 and in your Personal Plan 11: Achievements Extended. You have already completed short achievement statements for each.

Convert these short statements or bullet point statements into short sentences for your Foundation Resume:

-

-

-

-

These become part of your overall Foundation Resume, related to a specific profession.

Job-specific criteria

Job-specific criteria and skills required are listed in the criteria for a particular job.

These job-specific criteria have already been identified in Chapter 11: Achievements Extended and in your Personal Plan 11: Achievements Extended. You have already completed short achievement statements for each.

Convert these short statements or bullet point statements into short sentences for your Foundation Resume:

-

-

-

-

Personal achievements

These may be added personal achievements from other activities you have done. They are selected achievements that relate to a specific job; for example, a role in a sporting organisation, volunteer activities, part-time roles or other awards.

These personal aspects were identified and developed in your Personal Plan: Achievements Extended. You have already completed short achievement statements for each.

These are personal factors that you feel relate directly to the specific job. They are added qualities you may have that can help make you stand out.

If none come to mind, then do not worry. It is better to just omit this part, rather than try to concoct something that does not provide a further link between yourself and the job.

Convert these short statements or bullet point statements into short sentences for your Foundation Resume.

-

-

These will be part of your overall resume, when they relate directly to the job requirements.

Referees

- Contact name and position   Contact number

- Contact name and position   Contact number

- Contact name and position   Contact number

Do not forget to ask your choice of referees if they are willing to give you a good reference, before using their name.

Appendix

Personal Plan 14 – Targeted Resume (county format)

This relates to Chapter 15: Preparing your Targeted Resume: country-specific.

This part of your Personal Plan is to adapt your resume material into the final layout commonly used for your target country and region. It is an editing and reformatting process.

It uses the material you have complied in your Personal Plan for your Foundation Resume. It contains a wealth of resources about your qualifications and skills. The process is about selecting and editing the key material you want into your Targeted Resume.

In Chapter 15, you have identified key resume formats. Examples are given in the eResources for this book. A wide range of options for different countries are available on the web, including resume templates. Select the resume template that is appropriate to your country and region.

Approach

- Select a suitable format for your Targeted Resume (country).
  Resume template options include:

  o Resume examples in this book.

  o Free resume templates from many university websites and career advice centres.

  o Resume templates from a job search agency.

  o Free resume template from YouExec.

- In some cases, the resume format will be specified by the organisation. These are usually an online submission format or template.

- Work through the selected format headings. Copy and edit in your resume details from your Foundation Resume.

- This new Targeted Resume applies to a particular job. As you apply for different jobs with different job criteria you will create new versions of your Targeted Resume. Label the file names so that you can re-use and easily adapt them to a new job application.

Action

- Now complete the compilation of your Targeted Resume by selecting and editing details from your Foundation Resume into your Targeted Resume format.

Reference: eResources link for this book

For added resources and digital files related to this chapter:

- Search: Routledge Text Books or go to: www.routledge.com/
  Search window: type "Your Career", which will take you to the eResources for this book.
  Alternatively, you can use the short cut: https://tinyurl.com/kyxnfaq

    Then go to either:

- Appendices <TAB> Resources <TAB> (Appendices: Resources); or
- Templates <TAB> and the range of resume options.

Appendix
Personal Plan 15 – cover letter

This relates to Chapter 16: Preparing your tailored cover letter.
Examples of cover letters are provided in:

- Appendix Resources 7: Cover letter example 1.
- Appendix Resources 8: Cover letter example 2.

Complete the key points for your cover letter. Brainstorm short responses for the bullet points below:

- Indicate a strong interest in the advertised position (one sentence).
    - o

- Briefly summarise your main skills and qualifications (it can be a short sentence or bullet points).
    - o

    - o

    - o

- Have statements that link your abilities to the most significant job criteria.
  At this stage of planning, you may not have specific job criteria that you can address. In the interim, use two general criteria that would relate

to your chosen profession, for example, it could be analytical skills or communication skills.

  o

  o

  o

- Include an extra sentence to say that your skills and qualifications will contribute to the organisation.

  o

- Reference your attached resume for further details.

  o

- Welcome the opportunity for an interview for the role.

  o

These components can be used to compile your cover letter for your job application.

  With successive job applications you will end up with a number of variations to your cover letter. Each one is modified to relate to the requirements of the particular job and organisation.

Glossary

Body language: Ways we communicate with our body posture or voice tone. It is about the significance of posture and tone over the words we say.

Cover letter: A letter that accompanies a job application (and resume or CV).

CV: Curriculum Vitae. An outline of a person's skills, education, references and contact details. It is used in job applications to outline an applicant's suitability for a position. Also called a resume. In some countries, CV refers to a longer resume for academic positions.

Decision support: An analysis technique to weigh up decisions.

Email: Electronic communication via the Internet. Each user has their own address (email address) that allows messages (emails) to and from others.

Europass: A European Union (EU) approach to introduce a common resume or CV format for the EU.

Facebook: A free social network service that uses the Internet. It is the company that provides the service. It allows users to communicate, upload photos and videos, send messages and connect with others.

Force field analysis: An analysis technique to weigh up decisions and influencing factors.

Google Plus: A social media service from Google. It allows users to communicate, upload photos and videos, send messages and connect with others.

LinkedIn: A networking tool and website service that focuses on careers and jobs. It is a business- and employment-oriented social networking service.

Myers-Briggs®: An evaluation methodology for a person's personality type. It is a self-reporting type questionnaire that indicates different psychological preferences on how people perceive the world and make decisions.

Profile: An outline of a person's skills, education and experience. Also called a bio.

Referees or references: People who will provide recommendations about your skills or work experience. Usually included in resumes or CVs.

Resume: An outline of a person's skills, education, references and contact details. It is used in job applications to outline an applicant's suitability for a position. Also called a CV or Curriculum Vitae.

Skype®: An Internet communication tool that allows users to speak to each other live. It allows both video and audio calls.

Social media: Websites dedicated to electronic communications with a social aspect. They allow communication and sharing of information. They include Facebook, Twitter and Google Plus.

Spreadsheet: A computer programme that allows information to be entered, displayed and analysed in tabular form (rows and columns).

STRONG (Interest Inventory (SII))®: A psychological technique that analyses a person's interests.

SWOT: An analysis technique that evaluates strengths, weakness, opportunities and threats.

Tinyurl: www.tinyurl.com is a website that provides access to other websites via a short website url rather than a cumbersome, lengthy one.

Twitter: An online news and social networking service. It allows users to send short messages called 'tweets'.

url: Uniform resource locator. Also called a web address. It allows links via the World Wide Web or Internet. Usually http:// followed by a hostname such as www.example.com and this can be followed by a filename. A url can be: www.example.com/index.html

Word: Microsoft® software and format for digital word processing. Widely used across many software systems.

Index

CPSIA information can be obtained
at www.ICGtesting.com
Printed in the USA
LVOW13s1615170418
573808LV00003B/160/P